LIFE STAGES FINANCIAL GUIDES

The Divorce Money Map

TAKING CONTROL OF YOUR FINANCES BEFORE, DURING, AND AFTER DIVORCE

DONNA JEAN KENDRICK CFP®, CDFA®

HIGHLANDER
PRESS

CHECKOUT DONNA'S BACKGROUND ON FINRA'S BROKERCHECK
This book is designed to provide accurate and authoritative information on the subjects covered. It is not, however, intended to provide specific legal, tax, or other professional advice. For specific professional assistance, the services of an appropriate professional should be sought.

Securities offered through Cetera Financial Specialists LLC, member FINRA/SIPC. Advisory services offered through Cetera Investment Advisers LLC. Cetera firms are under separate ownership from any other named entity. 314 Washington Lane, Jenkintown, PA 19046.

The views stated in this book are not necessarily the opinion of Cetera Financial Specialists LLC and should not be construed directly or indirectly as an offer to buy or sell any securities mentioned herein. Due to volatility within the markets mentioned, opinions are subject to change without notice. Information is based on sources believed to be reliable; however, their accuracy or completeness cannot be guaranteed. Past performance does not guarantee future results.

ISBN: 978-1-956442-64-9

Published by Highlander Press
501 W. University Pkwy, Ste. B2
Baltimore, MD 21210

Cover and interior design: Hanne Broter
Author photo: Sarah Miller

Ordering Information: Special discounts are available on quantity purchases.

CONTENTS

PROLOGUE

In the summer of 2026, I hiked the trails of Sedona with two dear friends from my Philadelphia childhood. One still lives near me on the East Coast, while the other now calls the West Coast home. The year before, when we all turned fifty, we met in Sedona to celebrate. A year later, when I returned for a writers' retreat, it only seemed natural to rally my friends for "Sedona Round Two."

The resort was spectacular—breathtaking views nestled beside Cathedral Rock, one of Sedona's famed feminine vortices. On our first morning, armed with sunscreen (two of us are pale blondes braving the Arizona sun) and water bottles, we set off on what felt less like a hike and more like a pilgrimage. At the summit, after building a small rock cairn in homage, we paused to reflect.

There, we met two sisters from the Midwest, visiting during a family reunion. In casual conversation, the younger sister confided that this climb was especially meaningful, as her older sister was contemplating divorce. My friends quickly chimed in, pointing out that I was in the midst of writing a book about navigating finances during divorce—the very reason we had returned to Sedona. What began as small talk deepened into something more. Numbers were exchanged, and text threads began.

After the sisters departed, one of my friends and I fell into our own heartfelt conversation. She shared her personal experience with divorce in California—a very different process than in Pennsylvania. What struck me most, however, wasn't the legal or logistical side of her story. Instead, it was the emotional road map: the grief of a broken heart, the loss of future dreams, the financial crossroads, and the sheer determination to create a new life.

This is her story—in her own words—that she felt called to share with the readers of this guidebook:

> *The moment I saw the text from my soon-to-be ex-husband, my stomach dropped. I raced to my vice principal's office, barely managing to string together a few words to request the rest of the day off.*
>
> *I had to get home—to find a credit card I desperately needed to cancel before he could do more financial damage.*

When the credit card company told me I couldn't close the account without the physical card in hand—even though my name and Social Security number were on it—I felt powerless. My income had helped build that credit line, but now I was locked out of protecting myself. It was just one moment in a storm of many, but it marked the beginning of my journey to reclaim control.

Within days of learning about the infidelity, I'd packed up and moved out of our shared home. With barely anything to start over, I landed in a rental near the local university—surrounded by noisy frat houses, enduring brutal summer heat without air conditioning, and trying to piece together a new life. I didn't know what documents I needed, what to ask, or where to begin.

That sense of disorientation, of being swallowed by uncertainty, is why this workbook exists.

You don't have to wander through this alone. Whether you're just beginning to consider divorce or you're deep in the process, this book is your guide, your anchor, and your road map.

You can do this. And when you come out the other side, you won't just have survived—you'll have grown stronger, wiser, and more in control of your future.

Start here.

INTRODUCTION

Hello, I'm Donna Jean Kendrick. We may have just met, but I'm going to go ahead and ask for your trust.

This book wasn't supposed to be here yet. Originally, I was supposed to be writing the third book in my Life Stages Financial Guides series, scheduled for 2026. But the universe—pesky, insistent, and sometimes sarcastic—had other plans.

During my neatly scheduled business planning time in early 2025, that little voice in my head would not shut up:

- "People are divorcing now."
- "They're scared, confused, overwhelmed."
- "They need help today—not in two years."

I wanted to argue. I'm already wearing plenty of hats: Certified Financial Planner® (CFP), Certified Divorce Financial Analyst ® (CDFA), business owner, podcaster, wife, mom to a blended gaggle of six kids, and dog mom to both a 161-pound nine-year-old Newfoundland and a doodle who refuses to get with the potty-training program (a.k.a. *my husband's dog*). Adding another project to my plate felt like madness.

But when the universe speaks—repeatedly—you eventually listen. I finally emailed my publisher (a goddess in human form who somehow makes schedules bend to her will) to ask if we could move this book forward. By the end of the day, she'd reshuffled everything to make it possible.

So, there I was, Fourth of July vacation, pen in hand, loose-leaf paper spread across a picnic table by a brook, swatting mosquitoes and pretending it was all very idyllic. I wrote. I crossed things out. I stared at the water. And … nothing came.

Instead, what arrived was another divine download, complete with sarcasm: "DJ, stop writing the book you *planned*. Write the book people actually need. You're a Philly girl—give it to them straight. Make it something they can dig into when the world is spinning."

And that's when I realized: this wasn't supposed to be a traditional book at all. This was supposed to be a *guide*. Something hands-on. Something practical. A workbook, not a dusty volume.

Naturally, I did what any good researcher does—I ordered nearly every divorce planner Amazon Prime could deliver in forty-eight hours. The results were … educational:

- One binder was well thought out, complete with folders, Ziploc envelopes, and pages for emotional work.
- Another felt like a battle manual, crammed with war metaphors and blank pages to track your ex's every misstep. (I get it, but wow—intense.)
- And one was clearly written by either AI or an intern distracted by TikTok: It actually advised, *"Remove the glue from your false eyelashes."*

So, after laughing, groaning, and shaking my head, I knew exactly what this workbook needed to be. Something you could carry with you—tote bag, briefcase, or even in the car when you need a private moment to take a call. Big enough for real writing space (because let's be honest, the average age of divorce often coincides with the average age of needing readers).

This isn't a book to sit on a shelf and collect dust. It's a companion. It's meant to travel with you through one of the hardest transitions of your life—giving you structure when everything feels chaotic, and encouragement when the weight feels unbearable.

My *why?* It's you. You deserve clarity. You deserve support. You deserve confidence. So, here we are. Me, inviting you to grab a pen (bonus points for colorful ones—I love the way ink changes with pressure, and yes, I'll ask you to do this too). Get ready to write, scratch out, doodle, emphasize, and maybe even run your fingers over the pages when you need to feel grounded.

Let's begin.

HOW TO USE THIS BOOK

Really? Who needs instructions on how to read a book? To be honest—you do. The world is swirling right now. This workbook/guide is here to help you organize, strategize, and, honestly, to gain some control during this roller coaster of change. Here's how I suggest you use these pages:

1. **Carve out thirty minutes of quiet time** and review the pages. Yes, I know "quiet time" is a luxury. You might still be living with your soon-to-be ex. If you have young kids, your only peace may be sitting in the SUV between baseball and lacrosse practice. Wherever you find it, be intentional. Review the pages so your subconscious begins mapping the process. Trust me—lean into it. It works.

2. **Start at the very beginning.** Think of this as creating your own treasure map. (If you grew up in the '70s and '80s like I did, it's kind of like a Choose Your Own Adventure book—with an added layer of stress, courtesy of divorce.) Let's try to make a game of it so the process feels less heavy. Begin with the Personal Document Locator Predivorce. Highlight blank sections so you can easily spot what's missing and fill them in later. This is the first step in building your Financial Road Map—soon to be known as your Divorce Map.

3. **Use the workbook.** This workbook was designed in 8 × 10 format, so you have room to write. Stay organized, my new friend. If you have the bad habit of printing out documents or statements and tucking them in between the pages, please do so but fold in half and tape to the inseam so these private pages don't fall out. Or, use a paperclip.

4. **Work through the sections in order.** For many, this is the first rodeo. Others may have watched friends go through a divorce. And for some (like my mom), it might be a second or third time. No matter your experience, these pages walk you through the journey at a steady pace. Trust that by following along, you'll gather the correct information, reach the right people, and present your financials during discovery in an organized, thoughtful way.

5. **Stop only at natural pauses—not procrastination points.** Some divorces can be finalized in ninety days. Others take a year. Some drag on much longer. If you're like me, you'll want to power through all the pages and be done—but divorce doesn't always move that way. Think back to that treasure map or Choose Your Own Adventure analogy: Sometimes you get the big "X" at the end, and sometimes you loop back to Phase 2. When the process pauses, keep your workbook (and a pen and highlighter) close by so you're ready when new information comes.

6. **Gather your financial information early.** Collect details on accounts, insurance, benefits, etc. When you meet with your divorce attorney, let her know you're already working on what she'll call your financial affidavit. These pages exist to accelerate that process—and possibly save you hours in legal fees—because you'll already be prepared.

7. Model your financial settlement. Use the spending plan pages to test how different settlement offers affect your inflows and outflows. Review your net worth statement too—it's often a better indicator of your financial reality than annual income. Please don't skip this step; it can help you see your wholeness in a new way. If you're working with a CDFA®, financial planner, or accountant, lean on them to run scenarios and check for tax implications. (Spoiler: Not all money is created equal when taxes get involved.)

8. Move into the postdivorce section. Once the settlement is finalized and the judge signs off, this is your chance to fully understand your new you—on paper. This becomes the foundation for your next stage in life. Sit down with your financial planner to create your new Financial Road Map. Your Divorce Map evolves into your future plan. From here, you step into the opportunities waiting for you.

9. Dream again. The final chapter looks to your long-term goals. This is where you get to imagine your future. My own journey was through widowhood, not divorce. After Greg's passing, I never let myself dream. I lived in mourning, replaying the past instead of envisioning what could be. My biggest regret? I shut my soul off from living again because I thought dreaming was selfish. Learn from me—don't make that mistake. Use this space to dream big about the life you get to build.

"You can't control what God/Spirit does.
You can't control what someone else does.
You can only control what YOU do next."
—Unknown

Take this next step. You might just amaze yourself.

UNDERSTANDING DIVORCE: CORE CONCEPTS

Before we go any further, let's pause to get clear on a few core divorce concepts. Divorce law is state-specific, which means the rules that apply to your settlement depend on where you live. The process you choose will also shape your experience. These quick references will give you a foundation but remember: Your divorce attorney or professional is your best guide (see the chapter "Divorce Attorney Interview Questions").

The Five W's of Divorce

1. Who. Your team of trusted professionals should consist of the following:
- Divorce Lawyer Accountant/CPA
- Financial Planner/CDFA Credentials
- Therapist/Counselor
- Your Best Friend

2. What. Your divorce will culminate in what is commonly referred to as the settlement. The settlement comes in two parts: the financial and logistical. Both parts are permanent and impact your future. These pages will help you create a Divorce Map for your financials, which will help provide your attorney with the needed information so you can move forward with submitting your financial affidavit and negotiating a settlement.

That financial settlement will ultimately flow into and impact the logistics of your life postdivorce. Post divorce, this guide will help you create action steps for physically moving accounts, updating titles, beneficiaries, etc., as well as setting up the Financial Road Map for your new tomorrow so that you and your financial planner can use the new information as a launching point for establishing immediate goals, transitional goals, and long-term goals.

The future is bright, I promise.

3. When. There are calendar pages in the back of this book. Start using them as soon as possible and record the dates of meetings, correspondence, conversations, etc. Color coding may make this task easier. Life can feel very frantic and busy after the discussion of divorce takes over your everyday thoughts, and rightfully so. The today you know feels and looks different from yesterday, and the day before. Your head spins at times. We live our daily lives in the exhausting energy of fight or flight, a response our ancestors used to protect themselves from becoming prey. Yup, same brain triggers being used.

Start using the calendar pages to track events and appointments related to your divorce and make these pages your new go-to. Right now, turn to the back of this book and mark today's date with these words, "Divorce Map" and then highlight the words in green. This is your starting point for taking control of your finances and finding your next best day.

4. Where. In the next few pages, I'll explain to you how to use this book. You can use this workbook and complete the pages right here. Use this guide wherever you are, wherever you need it. It is here to help you navigate the whole divorce process, beginning, middle, and end.

5. Why. In my opinion, there are four major aspects to divorce: financial, emotional, legal, and logistical. This book focuses on the financial aspects. My goal is to support you in controlling and organizing your financial needs to help expedite the divorce process and save you time and money.

FINANCIAL

This planner will help you to:
- Get organized.
- Be confident.
- Take the next best step and use your time wisely.
- Know about what's next and have what you need at your fingertips when your legal counsel requests it.

EMOTIONAL

Please know this book is written with a ton of empathy, love, and good intentions for your heart, soul, and finances concurrently. I encourage you to lean on your best friend, a qualified life coach or psychological counselor, or peer support groups. I am a big fan of peer support, finding people like you who are going through the same thing. Sometimes a late-night call and a glass of good strong drink is needed, and, heck, the more the merrier in the world, Voxer, WhatsApp, and group texts. Be wary of telling the immediate family too much about the emotional side of your divorce because you might very well decide to stay with your spouse, and, at that point, judgments have most likely been made.

LEGAL

I am not an attorney or consider myself a guru of the Pennsylvania divorce code. I encourage you to find excellent representation aligned with your budget (the one time I will use the *b* word in this book).

A few years ago, a close family member—let's call her Shirley—was going through a divorce. Because I work closely with divorce attorneys as a CDFA®, she reached out to me for referrals. I gave her the names of three female attorneys I deeply respect. Instead of retaining one of them, Shirley decided to use the attorney provided through her work benefits.

That's when the trouble started. Under the group plan, she was allotted only a set number of hours. The process dragged. During that delay, her soon-to-be ex—let's call him Lenny—retained one of the attorneys I had originally recommended. When I heard, I cringed. That particular attorney is fair but shrewd. Gulp.

The divorce stretched on for nearly two years. To make matters worse, Shirley and Lenny continued to live under the same roof the entire time. Stress ran high, especially for their young adult children. (Side note: the house had only one bathroom. Yes, one. That commode became the epicenter of every argument—who got in, how long they stayed, and who clogged it. Honestly, Saturday Night Live *should make a sketch about it.)*

Part of the delay was Shirley's attorney, who simply wasn't a divorce specialist. She was often unavailable, pulled away by estate cases, DUIs, and even land disputes. Shirley found herself spending hours researching Pennsylvania divorce law and creating financial spreadsheets just to keep the process moving. Meanwhile, Lenny's attorney—who practiced only divorce law—kept everything on track, presenting thorough, justified financial offers and pushing forward with confidence.

By the end of it all, Shirley owed alimony, had to buy out Lenny's share of their home (which had quadrupled in value since they purchased it fifteen years earlier), and he walked away with 100 percent of his pension. Shirley was left struggling to keep up with alimony payments and the cost of maintaining the family home. Lenny, on the other hand, bought a small condo on the bay and now works happily from his desk with a water view.

Moral of the story: Get yourself strong representation. And when you're referred to a good divorce attorney, don't hesitate—because if you don't hire them, your spouse just might.

LOGISTICAL

We could rename this subsection "Real Estate, Mortgages, And Relocation." Yes, many moving parts happen after a divorce is settled, moving funds, retitling houses and cars, updating beneficiaries, etc. But the central logistical aspect to divorce you'll focus on in this workbook is answering the question, "Do I stay, or do I go?" In fact, there's an assessment in the next section to help you answer this core question.

In divorce, parties often have children, so being local for custody, staying in a specific school district, etc., are all essential logistical decisions. Affording a home, including a new or recharacterized mortgage, annual school and local taxes, and upkeep, is a major consideration.

I always remember the first snowstorm outside of Philadelphia after my husband Greg passed. I recall being thankful we had chosen a house with no sidewalk because all I had to do was shovel my driveway and walkway to our front door. Now that I am remarried with six kids and live in a large corner house, I constantly bitch (oops, another *b* word) about the time and energy it takes to shovel our pitched driveway and 200 yards of sidewalk.

Without fail, I come inside and strip off my insulated gloves to shake my finger at my new husband Jim and remind him that I have a life insurance policy on him so, should he "go," I can afford a seasonal contract for landscaping and shoveling the house.

If we ever divorce, I will undoubtedly add that cost into my expenses during our financial discovery (If you are reading this, Jim, love ya and have no plans to being your second divorce).

If you would like to learn more about Jim's first divorce and the lessons learned, please tune into our podcast together: *Widow, Wisdom, and Wealth®.* No matter what, Jim's first divorce often becomes a topic of discussion.

Types of Divorce

Here are some of the most common terms and processes you'll hear when discussing your options:

- **Collaborative Divorce:** A team-based approach where professionals—such as attorneys, financial specialists, CDFAs, divorce coaches, psychologists, or realtors—support the couple in reaching a settlement without going to court. The end goal is a legally binding agreement reviewed by a judge.
- **Arbitration:** An alternative dispute resolution (ADR) method where a qualified arbitrator hears the case outside of court. The arbitrator's decision is usually binding, eliminating the need for traditional court proceedings.
- **Mediation:** Another ADR method where a neutral mediator facilitates discussion to help the couple resolve issues. Unlike arbitration, the mediator does not issue a binding decision.
- **Equitable Distribution:** Assets are divided in a way that is fair, though not necessarily equal.
- **Community Property States:** In these states, property acquired during the marriage is generally divided fifty-fifty. States include Arizona, California, Idaho, Louisiana, Nevada, New Mexico, Texas, Washington, and Wisconsin.

PHASE ONE: BEFORE THE DIVORCE

IMMEDIATE ACTION STEPS

Divorce often catches one partner off guard. Maybe it happens during dinner in a public place, carefully chosen to avoid a scene. Or you come home from work to find that half of everything is gone.

A mom in our neighborhood once negotiated her divorce while still living under the same roof as her husband—neither could afford to move out. She pushed for a fifty-fifty split; he resisted, wanting to trade pension for house value. The conversations turned to weeks, months, and then a year went by, with hostility building day by day.

One winter evening, she came home from work, and the house looked darker than usual. When she opened the front door, she realized that half the dining room chairs were missing. As she moved to the living room, the sofa was there, but not the love seat and chair. Up to the bedroom: one lamp, one nightstand, one chest of drawers, and one pillow, all gone. Shampoo was on the shower shelf, but not the conditioner. A bar of Irish Spring soap was cleanly and intentionally cut in half.

Her husband agreed to her offer sarcastically and visually, taking 50 percent.
Oh, she had a roast in the crockpot—he took half of that, too!

Whether your divorce begins with a surprise or a mutual decision, the next step is logistics, especially financial ones. Often, one partner controls the log-ins, passwords, and accounts. The other feels vulnerable and overwhelmed about what to do next.

This checklist is here to change that. In the pages ahead, you'll find practical action steps to help you gather critical information and start protecting your financial future.

CHECKLIST

☐ **Pull your credit report at www.annualcreditreport.com.**
- Choose one report vendor (Experian, Equifax, TransUnion). * The goal is to run it again every three to four months.
- Contact any company that has presented information in the report that you want to dispute. Preferably, reach out in writing and maintain good, dated records of each correspondence.

☐ **Open a checking and savings account in your name.**

☐ **Inventory credit cards.**
- Remove name from joint accounts.
- Inquire about debt obligations.

☐ **Identify any joint accounts.**
- Print the most recent statements.
- If withdrawing funds, consider no more than half.
- Find out how to remove your name from the account.

☐ **Interview three divorce attorney referrals, see the chapter entitled "Interview Questions for Divorce Attorneys."**

☐ **Interview three financial planners, see the chapter entitled "Interview Questions for Financial Planners."**

☐ **Complete the chapter entitled "Predivorce Personal Document Locator."**

☐ **Complete the chapter entitled "Premarital Asset Inventory."**

☐ **Complete the chapter entitled "Predivorce Asset & Liability Inventory."**
- Beneficiary confirmation.
- Life insurance: Obtain a copy of the original documents or the most recent statement showing the same.
- Retirement Funds.
  - Obtain a copy of the most recent statement showing the beneficiary designations.
  - Research to see if a spousal waiver is needed to update beneficiaries.

☐ **Complete the chapter entitled "Flows of Income Worksheet."**

☐ **Complete the chapter entitled "Benefits Inventory."**

☐ **Additional Action Items.**

NOTES

THE IMPORTANCE OF BEING ORGANIZED

An essential part of managing your finances is keeping your financial records organized. Whether it's a utility bill to show proof of residency or a Social Security card for wage reporting purposes, there may be times when you need to locate a financial record or document—and you'll need to locate it relatively quickly. By taking the time to clear out and organize your financial records, you'll be able to find what you need exactly when you need it.

What Should You Keep?

If you tend to keep stuff because you "might need it someday," your desk or home office is probably overflowing with nonessential documents. One of the first steps in getting organized it to determine what records to keep, is to ask yourself, "Why do I need to keep this?" Documents you should keep are likely to be those that are difficult to obtain, such as:

- Tax returns
- Legal contracts
- Insurance claims
- Proof of identity

On the other hand, if you have documents and records that are easily duplicated elsewhere, such as online banking and credit card statements, you probably do not need to keep paper copies of the same information.

How Long Should You Keep Your Records?

Generally, a good rule of thumb is to keep financial records and documents only as long as necessary. For example, you may want to keep ATM and credit card receipts only temporarily, until you've reconciled them with your bank and/or credit card statement. On the other hand, if a document is legal and/or difficult to replace, you'll want to keep it for a more extended period or even indefinitely.

Some financial records may have more specific timetables. For example, the IRS generally recommends that taxpayers keep federal tax returns and supporting documents for a minimum of three years, up to seven years after the date of filing. Certain circumstances may even warrant keeping your tax records indefinitely. Listed below are some recommendations on how long to keep specific documents.

Records to keep for one year or less:
- Bank or credit union statements
- Credit card statements
- Utility bills
- Auto and homeowners' insurance policies

Records to keep for more than a year:
- Tax returns and supporting documentation
- Mortgage contracts
- Property appraisals
- Annual retirement and investment statements
- Receipts for major purchases and home improvements

Records to keep indefinitely:
- Birth, death, and marriage certificates
- Adoption records
- Citizenship and military discharge papers
- Social Security card

Keep in mind that the above recommendations are general guidelines, and your personal circumstances may warrant keeping these documents for shorter or longer periods of time.

Out with the Old, In with the New

An easy way to prevent paperwork from piling up is to remember the phrase "out with the old, in with the new." For example, when you receive this year's auto insurance policy, discard the one from last year. When you receive your annual investment statement, discard the monthly or quarterly statements you've been keeping. In addition, review your files at least once a year to keep your filing system on the right track.

Finally, when you are ready to get rid of certain records and documents, don't just throw them in the garbage. To protect sensitive information, you should invest in a good-quality, crosscut shredder to destroy your documents, especially if they contain Social Security numbers, account numbers, or other personal information.

Where Should You Keep Your Records?

You could go the traditional route and use a simple set of labeled folders in a file drawer. More important documents should be kept in a fire-resistant file cabinet, safe, or safe-deposit box.

If space is tight and you need to reduce clutter, you might consider electronic storage for some of your financial records. You can save copies of online documents or scan documents and convert them to electronic form. You'll want to keep backup copies on a portable storage device or hard drive and make sure that your computer files are secure.

You could also use a cloud storage service that encrypts your uploaded information and stores it remotely. If you use cloud storage, make sure to use a reliable company that has a good reputation and offers automatic backup and technical support.

Once you've found a place to keep your records, it may be helpful to organize and store them according to specific categories (e.g., banking, insurance, proof of identity), which will make it even easier to access what you might need.

Consider Creating a Personal Document Locator

Another option for organizing your financial records is to create a Personal Document Locator, which is simply a detailed list of where you have stored your financial records. This list can be helpful whenever you are trying to locate a specific document. It can also assist your loved ones in locating your financial records in the event of an emergency. Typically, a Personal Document Locator will include the following information:

- Personal information.
- Personal contacts (e.g., attorney, tax preparer, and financial advisor).
- Online accounts with usernames and passwords.
- List of specific locations of important documents (e.g., home, office, safe).

WHAT TO GATHER CHECKLIST

☐ **Birth Certificates**
  - Yourself
  - Children

☐ **Veterans** eligible for burial benefits: www.va.gov

☐ **Social Security Cards**
  - Yourself
  - Children

☐ **Marriage Certificate**

☐ **Prenuptial Agreements**

☐ **Divorce Decrees**

☐ **Military Discharge Paperwork**
  - To obtain copies, contact the National Archives and Records Administration at https://www.archives.gov/.

☐ **Citizenship Papers**

☐ **Burial Contracts**

☐ **Death Certificates**

☐ **Organ Donor Form**

☐ **Deed To Your Home**

☐ **Deed to any other properties held in your spouse's name**

☐ **Bank Documents**
  - Yourself
  - Children

☐ **Safe-Deposit Box Key**

☐ **Mortgage Documents**

☐ **Title to cars, boats, etc.**

☐ **Auto Loans/Leases**

☐ **Estate Documents**
- Will
- Living Will
- Power of Attorney (POA)
- Trusts

☐ **Insurance Policies**
- Automotive
- Home
- Umbrella
- Disability
- Life (term and permanent)
- Health
- Long-Term Care
- Annuities

☐ **Employer retirement plan paperwork e.g., 401(k), 403(b), employer stock options**

☐ **Personal retirement savings e.g., Traditional IRA, Roth IRA, annuities**

☐ **Investment/brokerage accounts e.g., mutual funds, stocks, bonds**

☐ **Tax Returns (two years)**

☐ **Business Partnership Agreements**

☐ **List of Credit Cards**

☐ **List of Utilities**

☐ **List of Bill Payers on file (start a calendar of due dates)**

☐ **List of Assets (e.g., art, jewelry, personal property)**

☐ **List of School Contacts (if you have children)**

☐ **List of Medical Practitioners**
- Yourself
- Children

NOTES

NOTES

PREDIVORCE PERSONAL DOCUMENT LOCATOR

Please keep in a secure location!

This Personal Document Locator is simply a detailed list of where you store your important records and papers, and who your primary adviser and contacts are. This list will assist your loved ones in the event of your death or disability. Keep this list at home along with your other important documents, and make sure a trusted family member knows where it is, or provide a copy to the family member, your executor, and/or your attorney. Remember to update your Personal Document Locator at least once a year to ensure its accuracy.

PART A. PERSONAL INFORMATION

Name (First, Middle, Last):

Street Address:

City, State, Zip:

Social Security Number:

Date of Birth:

Place of Birth:

PART B. PERSONAL CONTACTS

Divorce Attorney

Name:

Firm Name:

Street Address:

City, State, Zip:

Office Phone:

Mobile Phone:

Email:

Website:

Billing Contact:

Paralegal

Name:

Firm Name:

Street Address:

City, State, Zip:

Office Phone:

Mobile Phone:

Email:

Website:

Billing Contact:

Accountant

Name:

Firm Name:

Street Address:

City, State, Zip:

Office Phone:

Mobile Phone:

Email:

Website:

Billing Contact:

Insurance Agent - Property and Casualty

Name:

Firm Name:

Street Address:

City, State, Zip:

Office Phone:

Mobile Phone:

Email:

Website:

Billing Contact:

Insurance Agent - Life

Name:

Firm Name:

Street Address:

City, State, Zip:

Office Phone:

Mobile Phone:

Email:

Website:

Billing Contact:

Financial adviser

Name:

Firm Name:

Street Address:

City, State, Zip:

Office Phone:

Mobile Phone:

Email:

Website:

Billing Contact:

Real Estate Agent

Name:

Firm Name:

Street Address:

City, State, Zip:

Office Phone:

Mobile Phone:

Email:

Website:

Billing Contact:

Mortgage Broker

Name:

Company Name:

Street Address:

City, State, Zip:

Office Phone:

Mobile Phone:

Email:

Website:

Billing Contact:

Estate Attorney

Name:

Firm Name:

Street Address:

City, State, Zip:

Office Phone:

Mobile Phone:

Email:

Website:

Billing Contact:

Counselor (Yours)

Name: ....

Company Name: ....

Street Address: ....

City, State, Zip: ....

Office Phone: ....

Mobile Phone: ....

Email: ....

Website: ....

Billing Contact: ....

Counselor (Children)

Name: ....

Company Name: ....

Street Address: ....

City, State, Zip: ....

Office Phone: ....

Mobile Phone: ....

Email: ....

Website: ....

Billing Contact: ....

Online Accounts

Consider use of online password aggregator!

WEBSITE	USERNAME	PASSWORD

WEBSITE	USERNAME	PASSWORD

NOTES

PART C. LOCATION KEY

Specify the location(s) where you keep your documents (e.g., home, office, safe).

For each item in Part D, write in the number in the box that corresponds to the correct location.

Location 1:

Location 2:

Location 3:

Location 4:

Location 5:

Location 6:

Location 7:

Location 8:

PART D. IMPORTANT DOCUMENTS

	LOCATION KEY
Will	
Durable Power of Attorney	
Health-Care Directives	
Trust Agreements	
Social Security Card	
Marriage Certificate	
Military Papers	
Divorce/Separation Papers	
Vehicle Titles	
Deeds	
Safe-Deposit Box/Keys	
Bank Account Records (e.g., checking and savings accounts, CDs)	
Tax Returns	
Mortgage and Loan Papers	
Insurance Policies: Home and Vehicles	
Insurance Policies: Property and Casualty	
Insurance Policies: Life	
Insurance Policies: Health	
Business Papers (e.g., incorporation papers, trademarks, and patents)	
Retirement Account Papers (e.g., IRAs, and annuities)	
Investment Papers (e.g., securities, stocks, bonds, mutual funds)	
Proof of Citizenship	
Important Keys	
Antiques and Heirlooms	
Jewelry	
Cash	
Funeral Instructions (e.g., cemetery plot deed, and burial instructions)	

NOTES

NOTES

FINDING A DIVORCE ATTORNEY

Of all the attorneys that I have worked with over the years as a certified divorce financial analyst (CDFA®), only one had a master's degree in finance as well as his law degree. I was impressed by his ability to look ahead at the quality of money and how it would impact his clients today as well as their new tomorrow. He was heart-centered and no frills at the same time. He seemed to have his clients' best interests at heart, and he educated them along the way. Often, money may be taxable or non-taxable (deemed for retirement). You may hear your financial planner also refer to this as qualified versus nonqualified money.

This attorney was skilled in modeling how funds may be needed in the future versus the taxable implications of taking funds now. For example, if a divorcée keeps the family home because he wants the kids not to be unsettled and his alimony stops in the agreed-upon seven years, will he still be able to afford the mortgage? Is there enough liquid cash to cover any emergency improvements, like a roof that was supposed to last twenty-five years, but started leaking rainwater into your living room at year fifteen? If our client had accepted a majority of retirement funds in exchange for equity in the house, he might have to pay taxes and a
10 percent early withdrawal penalty on the replacement roof funds.

Making sense? The moral of the story: Make sure your attorney is savvy in the financial aspect of educating you on the quality of money during your negotiations. If not, ask if he or she works with a CDFA® to help guide you through this side of the agreement.

Interview Questions

DIVORCE ATTORNEY INTERVIEW #1

Date: **Time:**   **Location:**

Basic Information

Name:

Company Name:

Address 1:

Address 2:

City:

State:

Zip:

Office Phone:

Cell Phone:

Email:

Administrative Assistant Email:

Office Hours:

Visit Types:

☐ Office

☐ Virtual

☐ Home

Professional Qualifications

Education:

Licenses :

States:

Counties:

How many years in practice:

At this firm:

Percentage of cases that go to trial vs. settlement:

Practice

Practice Team

  # of employees:

  # of lawyers on staff

  # of office support

Niche or Practice Specialty:

Costs

Retainer: Yes ☐ No ☐

Details:

Hourly Fee:

Administrative charges (copies, phone calls, etc.):

Do you have other people who work on the case with you?

How am I charged for those services?

Payment Plans: Yes ☐ No ☐

Types of Payments Accepted:

☐ Credit Card

☐ American Express

☐ Discover

☐ Checks

☐ ACH

☐ Physical

Communication

Visit frequency:

Email frequency:

Call frequency:

Best method of communication:

My Role:

Explain the expected stages and timeline for my case:

Interview Questions

DIVORCE ATTORNEY INTERVIEW #2

Date: **Time:**   **Location:**

Basic Information

Name:

Company Name:

Address 1:

Address 2:

City:

State:

Zip:

Office Phone:

Cell Phone:

Email:

Administrative Assistant Email:

Office Hours:

Visit Types:

☐ Office

☐ Virtual

☐ Home

Professional Qualifications

Education:

Licenses:

States:

Counties:

How many years in practice:

At this firm:

Percentage of cases that go to trial vs. settlement:

Practice

Practice Team

Number of employees:

Number of lawyers on staff:

Number of office support:

Niche or practice specialty:

Costs

Retainer: Yes ☐ No ☐

Details:

Hourly Fee:

Administrative charges (copies, phone calls, etc.):

Do you have other people who work on the case with you?

How am I charged for those services?

Payment Plans: Yes ☐ No ☐

Types of Payments Accepted:

☐ Credit Card

☐ American Express

☐ Discover

☐ Checks

☐ ACH

☐ Physical

Communication

Visit frequency:

Email frequency:

Call frequency:

Best method of communication:

My Role:

Explain the expected stages and timeline for my case:

Interview Questions

DIVORCE ATTORNEY INTERVIEW #3

Date: **Time:**   **Location:**

Basic Information

Name:

Company Name:

Address 1:

Address 2:

City:

State:

Zip:

Office Phone:

Cell Phone:

Email:

Administrative Assistant Email:

Office Hours:

Visit Types:

☐ Office

☐ Virtual

☐ Home

Professional Qualifications

Education:

Licenses:

States:

Counties:

How many years in practice:

At this firm:

Percentage of cases that go to trial vs. settlement:

Practice

Practice Team

Number of employees:

Number of lawyers on staff:

Numberof office support

Niche or practice specialty:

Costs

Retainer: Yes ☐ No ☐

Details:

Hourly Fee:

Administrative charges (copies, phone calls, etc.):

Do you have other people who work on the case with you?

How am I charged for those services?

Payment Plans: Yes ☐ No ☐

Types of Payments Accepted:

☐ Credit Card

☐ American Express

☐ Discover

☐ Checks

☐ ACH

☐ Physical

Communication

Visit frequency:

Email frequency:

Call frequency:

Best method of communication:

My Role:

Explain the expected stages and timeline for my case:

NOTES

NOTES

FINANCIAL ADVISER INTERVIEW QUESTIONS

FINANCIAL ADVISER INTERVIEW #1

Date: **Time:**   **Location:**

Basic Information

Name:

Address:

Phone:

Email:

Website

Location:

Do they offer virtual visits/in-person visits?

What are their office hours?

Professional Qualifications:

Education:

Certifications :

☐ Certified Financial Planner®

☐ CDFA

Licenses:

☐ Series 6, 7, 22, 57, 79, 82, 86/87, 99, 4, 9/10, 14, 16, 23, 24, 26, 27, 28, 39, 50, 51, 52, 53, 54, 3, 30, 31, 32, 34, 63, 65, 66 (Circle all that apply; information may be available on the professional's website.)

☐ Federal (FINRA-Financial Industry Regulatory Authority)

☐ State(s) (SEC-U.S. Security Exchange Commission)

Life Insurance Licenses:

☐ Disability Insurance

☐ Health Insurance

☐ Property and Casualty Insurance

☐ Long-Term Care Insurance

☐ Life Insurance

How many years in practice?

Independent:

Sole Proprietor:

Team Based:

Group Based:

Is there an asset minimum?

What services are offered?

☐ Financial planning

☐ Asset management

☐ Portfolio review and evaluation

☐ Access to financial planning tools

☐ Cash flow analysis

☐ Retirement account investment analysis and allocation (401(k), 403(b), etc.)

☐ Budgeting

☐ Education funding planning

☐ Estate analysis and planning

☐ Risk management analysis (i.e., insurance policy review)

☐ Behavioral coaching and wealth mentoring

☐ Organization of client documents

Frequency of services:

☐ Onetime

☐ Ongoing

☐ Frequency of contact (semi-annual, annual review, email and call limits, etc.)

Cost and how they will get paid:

☐ Fee-Based (ongoing or onetime)

☐ Fee Only

☐ Commissions

☐ Financial Planning Fee:

☐ Investment Fee Schedule:

☐ Subscription Fee:

☐ Hourly Fee:

Average age of clients:

Niche or practice specialty:

Do you and I have any conflicts of interest?

What do you expect from me as a client?

What information will you need from me to get started?

Next steps:

How often do we communicate?

Best method of communication?

NOTES

NOTES

FINANCIAL ADVISER INTERVIEW QUESTIONS

FINANCIAL ADVISOR INTERVIEW #2

Date: **Time:**   **Location:**

Basic Information

Name:

Address:

Phone:

Email:

Website

Location:

Do they offer virtual visits /in-person visits?

What are their office hours?

Professional Qualifications:

Education:

Certifications :

☐ Certified Financial Planner®

☐ CDFA

Licenses:

☐ Series 6, 7, 22, 57, 79, 82, 86/87, 99, 4, 9/10, 14, 16, 23, 24, 26, 27, 28, 39, 50, 51, 52, 53, 54, 3, 30, 31, 32, 34, 63, 65, 66 (Circle all that apply; information may be available on the professional's website.)

☐ Federal (FINRA-Financial Industry Regulatory Authority)

☐ State (s) (SEC-U.S. Security Exchange Commission)

Life Insurance Licenses:

☐ Disability Insurance

☐ Health Insurance

☐ Property and Casualty Insurance

☐ Long-Term Care Insurance

☐ Life Insurance

How many years in practice?

Independent:

Sole Proprietor:

Team Based:

Group Based:

Is there an asset minimum?

What services are offered?

- ☐ Financial planning
- ☐ Asset management
- ☐ Portfolio review and evaluation
- ☐ Access to financial planning tools
- ☐ Cash flow analysis
- ☐ Retirement account investment analysis and allocation (401(k), 403(b), etc.)
- ☐ Budgeting
- ☐ Education funding planning
- ☐ Estate analysis and planning
- ☐ Risk management analysis (i.e., insurance policy review)
- ☐ Behavioral coaching and wealth mentoring
- ☐ Organization of client documents

Frequency of services:

- ☐ Onetime
- ☐ Ongoing
- ☐ Frequency of contact (semi-annual, annual review, email and call limits, etc.)

Cost and how they will get paid:

- ☐ Fee-Based (ongoing or onetime)
- ☐ Fee Only
- ☐ Commissions
- ☐ Financial Planning Fee:
- ☐ Investment Fee Schedule:
- ☐ Subscription Fee:
- ☐ Hourly Fee:

Average age of clients:

Niche or practice specialty:

Do you and I have any conflicts of interest?

What do you expect from me as a client?

What information will you need from me to get started?

Next steps:

How often do we communicate?

Best method of communication?

NOTES

NOTES

FINANCIAL ADVISOR INTERVIEW QUESTIONS

FINANCIAL ADVISOR INTERVIEW #3

Date: **Time:**   **Location:**

Basic Information

Name:

Address:

Phone:

Email:

Website

Location:

Do they offer virtual visits /in-person visits?

What are their office hours?

Professional Qualifications:

Education:

Certifications :

☐ Certified Financial Planner®

☐ CDFA

Licenses:

☐ Series 6, 7, 22, 57, 79, 82, 86/87, 99, 4, 9/10, 14, 16, 23, 24, 26, 27, 28, 39, 50, 51, 52, 53, 54, 3, 30, 31, 32, 34, 63, 65, 66 (Circle all that apply; information may be available on the professional's website.)

☐ Federal (FINRA-Financial Industry Regulatory Authority)

☐ State (s) (SEC-U.S. Security Exchange Commission)

Life Insurance Licenses:

☐ Disability Insurance

☐ Health Insurance

☐ Property and Casualty Insurance

☐ Long-Term Care Insurance

☐ Life Insurance

How many years in practice?

Independent:

Sole Proprietor:

Team Based:

Group Based:

Is there an asset minimum?

What services are offered?

☐ Financial planning

☐ Asset management

☐ Portfolio review and evaluation

☐ Access to financial planning tools

☐ Cash flow analysis

☐ Retirement account investment analysis and allocation (401(k), 403(b), etc.)

☐ Budgeting

☐ Education funding planning

☐ Estate analysis and planning

☐ Risk management analysis (i.e., insurance policy review)

☐ Behavioral coaching and wealth mentoring

☐ Organization of client documents

Frequency of services:

☐ Onetime

☐ Ongoing

☐ Frequency of contact (semi-annual, annual review, email and call limits, etc.)

Cost and how they will get paid:

☐ Fee-Based (ongoing or onetime)

☐ Fee Only

☐ Commissions

☐ Financial Planning Fee:

☐ Investment Fee Schedule:

☐ Subscription Fee:

☐ Hourly Fee:

Average age of clients:

Niche or practice specialty:

Do you and I have any conflicts of interest?

What do you expect from me as a client?

What information will you need from me to get started?

Next steps:

How often do we communicate?

Best method of communication?

NOTES

NOTES

ACCOUNTANT INTERVIEW QUESTIONS

ACCOUNTANT INTERVIEW #1

Date: **Time:**   **Location:**

Basic information:

Name:

Company Name:

Address 1:

Address 2:

City:

State:

Zip:

Office Phone:

Cell Phone:

Email:

Administrative Assistant Email:

Office Hours:

Visit Types:

☐ Office

☐ Virtual

☐ Home

Professional Qualifications:

Education:

Certifications:

C.P.A.:

Enrolled Agent:

Other:

How many years in practice:

At this firm:

Practice Model:

Practice Team

Number of employees:

Number of CPAs:

Number of Enrolled Agents:

Number of office support:

Expectation of visits and communication

☐ Annual

☐ Semi-annual

☐ Quarterly

☐ Monthly

☐ Email frequency:

☐ Call frequency:

☐ Best method of communication:

Average age of client base:

Niche or practice specialty:

Costs:

Onetime:

Subscription Fee:

Hourly Fee:

Payment Plans: Yes ☐ No ☐

Details:

Retainer: Yes ☐ No ☐

Types of Payments Accepted:

☐ Credit Card

☐ American Express

☐ Discover

☐ Checks

☐ ACH

☐ Physical

Communications:

Describe your onboarding practice.

What do you need, given that this is a divorce situation?

How best to get the information to you?

☐ Paper copies

☐ Portal upload

☐ Secure email

Postdivorce, how do we engage on an annual basis?

NOTES

NOTES

ACCOUNTANT INTERVIEW QUESTIONS

ACCOUNTANT INTERVIEW #2

Date: **Time:**   **Location:**

Basic information:

Name:

Company Name:

Address 1:

Address 2:

City:

State:

Zip:

Office Phone:

Cell Phone:

Email:

Administrative Assistant Email:

Office Hours:

Visit Types:

☐ Office

☐ Virtual

☐ Home

Professional Qualifications:

Education:

Certifications:

CPA:

Enrolled Agent:

Other:

How many years in practice:

At this firm:

Practice Model:

Practice Team

Number of employees:

Number of CPAs:

Number of Enrolled Agents:

Number of office support:

Expectation of visits and communication

☐ Annual

☐ Semi-annual

☐ Quarterly

☐ Monthly

☐ Email frequency:

☐ Call frequency:

☐ Best method of communication:

Average age of client base:

Niche or practice specialty:

Costs:

Onetime:

Subscription Fee:

Hourly Fee:

Payment Plans: Yes ☐ No ☐

Details:

Retainer: Yes ☐ No ☐

Types of Payments Accepted:

☐ Credit Card

☐ American Express

☐ Discover

☐ Checks

☐ ACH

☐ Physical

Communications:

Describe your onboarding practice.

What do you need, given that this is a divorce situation?

How best to get the information to you?

☐ Paper copies

☐ Portal upload

☐ Secure email

Postdivorce, how do we engage on an annual basis?

NOTES

NOTES

ACCOUNTANT INTERVIEW QUESTIONS

ACCOUNTANT INTERVIEW #3

Date: **Time:**   **Location:**

Basic information:

Name:

Company Name:

Address 1:

Address 2:

City:

State:

Zip:

Office Phone:

Cell Phone:

Email:

Administrative Assistant Email:

Office Hours:

Visit Types:

☐ Office

☐ Virtual

☐ Home

Professional Qualifications:

Education:

Certifications:

C.P.A.:

Enrolled Agent:

Other:

How many years in practice:

At this firm:

Practice model:

Practice Team

Number of employees:

Number of CPAs:

Number of Enrolled Agents:

Number of office support:

Expectation of visits and communication

☐ Annual

☐ Semi-annual

☐ Quarterly

☐ Monthly

☐ Email frequency:

☐ Call frequency:

☐ Best method of communication:

Average age of client base:

Niche or practice specialty:

Costs:

Onetime:

Subscription Fee:

Hourly Fee:

Payment Plans: Yes ☐ No ☐

Details:

Retainer: Yes ☐ No ☐

Types of Payments Accepted:

☐ Credit Card

☐ American Express

☐ Discover

☐ Checks

☐ ACH

☐ Physical

Communications:

Describe your onboarding practice.

What do you need, given that this is a divorce situation?

How best to get the information to you?

☐ Paper copies

☐ Portal upload

☐ Secure email

Postdivorce, how do we engage on an annual basis?

NOTES

NOTES

PREMARITAL ASSET INVENTORY

DESCRIPTION	OWNERSHIP	DATE OBTAINED	ORIGINAL VALUE	CURRENT VALUE

PREDIVORCE ASSET & LIABILITY INVENTORY

For ownership, please indicate Me, Spouse, or Joint.

Primary Residence

DESCRIPTION	OWNERSHIP	DATE OBTAINED	ORIGINAL VALUE	CURRENT VALUE

Secondary Properties

DESCRIPTION	OWNERSHIP	DATE OBTAINED	ORIGINAL VALUE	CURRENT VALUE

Vehicles

DESCRIPTION	OWNERSHIP	DATE OBTAINED	ORIGINAL VALUE	CURRENT VALUE

Boats

DESCRIPTION	OWNERSHIP	DATE OBTAINED	ORIGINAL VALUE	CURRENT VALUE

Artwork/Jewelry/Antiques

DESCRIPTION	OWNERSHIP	DATE OBTAINED	ORIGINAL VALUE	CURRENT VALUE

Life Insurance

DESCRIPTION	OWNERSHIP AND DISABILITY POLICIES	DATE OBTAINED	ORIGINAL VALUE	CURRENT VALUE

Long-Term Care Insurance

DESCRIPTION	OWNERSHIP	DATE OBTAINED	ORIGINAL VALUE	CURRENT VALUE

Vacation Pay

DESCRIPTION	OWNERSHIP	DATE OBTAINED	CURRENT VALUE

Individual Stocks

DESCRIPTION	ACCOUNT #	OWNERSHIP	COMPANY	ORIGINAL VALUE	CURRENT VALUE

Investment Brokerage Accounts

DESCRIPTION	ACCOUNT #	OWNERSHIP	COMPANY	CURRENT VALUE

Bonds (Corporate, Government, Municipal)

DESCRIPTION	ACCOUNT #	OWNERSHIP	COMPANY	CURRENT VALUE

Money Market Savings

DESCRIPTION	ACCOUNT #	OWNERSHIP	COMPANY	CURRENT VALUE

Checking

DESCRIPTION	ACCOUNT #	OWNERSHIP	COMPANY	CURRENT VALUE

Savings

DESCRIPTION	ACCOUNT #	OWNERSHIP	COMPANY	CURRENT VALUE

CDs

DESCRIPTION	ACCOUNT #	OWNERSHIP	DATE OF MATURITY	TERM AND PERCENTAGE	COMPANY	CURRENT VALUE

Retirement Savings in Your Name

Tax Deferred (401(k), 403(b), 457, Simple, SEP, IRA, Traditional IRA)

DESCRIPTION	ACCOUNT #	COMPANY	CURRENT VALUE

NOTES

529 Plans

DESCRIPTION	ACCOUNT #	COMPANY	CURRENT VALUE

Annuities

DESCRIPTION	ACCOUNT #	COMPANY	CURRENT VALUE

Trusts

DESCRIPTION	ACCOUNT #	COMPANY	CURRENT VALUE

Retirement Savings in Your Spouse's Name

DESCRIPTION	ACCOUNT #	COMPANY	CURRENT VALUE

Tax Free (401(k) Roth, 403(b) Roth, 457 Roth, Simple Roth IRA, SEP IRA Roth, Roth IRA)

DESCRIPTION	ACCOUNT #	COMPANY	CURRENT VALUE

529 Plans

DESCRIPTION	ACCOUNT #	COMPANY	CURRENT VALUE

Annuities

DESCRIPTION	ACCOUNT #	COMPANY	CURRENT VALUE

Employer Savings and Investments in Your Name
Stock Options

DESCRIPTION	ACCOUNT #	COMPANY	DATE OBTAINED	ORIGINAL VALUE	CURRENT VALUE

Restricted Stock Units

DESCRIPTION	ACCOUNT #	COMPANY	DATE OBTAINED	ORIGINAL VALUE	CURRENT VALUE

Employer Savings and Investments in Your Spouse's Name
Stock Options

DESCRIPTION	ACCOUNT #	COMPANY	DATE OBTAINED	ORIGINAL VALUE	CURRENT VALUE

Restricted Stock Units

DESCRIPTION	ACCOUNT #	COMPANY	DATE OBTAINED	ORIGINAL VALUE	CURRENT VALUE

FLOWS OF INCOME AND EXPENSES

Income

DESCRIPTION	GROSS INCOME TO DATE	OWNERSHIP	MONTHLY	ANNUAL
Employment				
Bonuses				
Investment Income				
Pensions				
Social Security				
Rental Income				
Disability Income				
Workers' Comp				
TOTAL				

Expenses

DESCRIPTION	LIABILITIES TO DATE	NECESSARY/ DISCRETIONARY	MONTHLY PAYMENT	ANNUAL PAYMENT
Mortgage/Rent				
HOA Fees				
Utilities				
Phone				
Cell Phone				
Internet				
Gas				
Electric				
Cable				
Trash				

Expenses

DESCRIPTION	LIABILITIES TO DATE	NECESSARY/ DISCRETIONARY	MONTHLY PAYMENT	ANNUAL PAYMENTY
Sewer				
Landscaping Mov/Plow				
Food				
Groceries				
Dining Out				
Transportation				
Car Payment				
Gas				
Repairs/ Maintenance				
Tolls				
Insurance				
Child Care				
Daycare				
Babysitters				
Education Expenses				
Sport Fees				
Credit Card				

Expenses

DESCRIPTION	LIABILITIES TO DATE	NECESSARY/ DISCRETIONARY	MONTHLY PAYMENT	ANNUAL PAYMENT
Loans				
Clothing				
Dry Cleaning				
Gym Membership				
Personal Care				
Insurance Premiums				
Health				
Dental				
Eye				
Life				

Expenses

DESCRIPTION	LIABILITIES TO DATE	NECESSARY/ DISCRETIONARY	MONTHLY PAYMENT	ANNUAL PAYMENT
Disability				
Short-Term				
Long-Term				
Umbrella				
Entertainment				
Streaming				
Subscriptions				
Conserts				
Movies				
Travel				
Gifts				
Pets				
Grooming				
Vet Care				
Charitable Giving				
Other				
TOTAL				

Yearly Summary

DESCRIPTION	MONTHLY	ANNUAL
Total Income		
Necessary Expenses		
Discretionary Expenses		
Overage/Underage		

NOTES

ENVELOPE SYSTEM

Here is how it works. There are twelve envelopes, white letter size 11.5 × 5 inches, white with the flap tucked in. On the top middle inside of each envelope, in colored marker, you write the title of each envelope.

Here are the twelve labels my mom used:

1. **Pizza** (Yes, my friends, our takeout only consisted of pizza on Friday nights. Correction: Pizza purchased with a coupon on Wednesday of "Buy One Get One" and frozen for Friday's "no meat" dinner)

2. **Gas**

3. **Gifts**

4. **Allowance-Marlene (my mom)**

5. **Allowance-Phil (my dad)**

6. **Groceries**

7. **Car Maintenance**

8. **Insurance**

9. **Church**

10. **Extra** There always seemed to be money here; my mom was strict about keeping to her budgeted amounts in the other envelopes. But, if there was a need to fund another category, we pulled money from this envelope. For example, if it was a holiday that we were hosting, so groceries would be higher, she would go to fund it from this envelope. If the amount in Extra grew too large from rolling over week to week, my mom would take about half of it out and hide it somewhere else, so it wouldn't get spent.

11. **Clothes**

12. **Utilities**

Once each envelope is created, put them in alphabetical order. Add the amount each envelope should contain under each title based on the set budget from the previous month's spend. Fill with appropriate amounts every week when paycheck is cashed (leaving mortgage amount in the checking account). Wrap all envelopes together with a large rubber band. Hide between the winter draperies in the upstairs hall closet.

*Reminder: Do not donate winter drapes without moving the "envelope system" first. Yes, readers, it happened.

Benefits inventory

Salary

Frequency of Pay

☐ Biweekly

☐ Every other week

☐ Once a month

Commission or Bonuses?

Pay Increases

☐ Guaranteed

☐ Merit or cost of living

☐ At review or annual?

☐ Nonqualified Deferred Compensation

These are benefits you may lose should you leave the employer. Many times, they are stock incentives for highly compensated employees to "make them sticky" to the job. (i.e., if they leave the company, they are leaving money on the table.)

Ability to Promote Upward

☐ Ask for your company's organizational chart.

Work Schedule

☐ Telecommuting?

☐ Flexible Hours? Core Hours?

☐ Mandatory Overtime?

☐ Travel?

Benefits

☐ **Short-Term Disability**

Waiting period

Percentage of coverage

☐ **Long-term Disability**

Waiting period

Percentage of coverage

Maximum Benefit

☐ **Life Insurance**

☐ Ability to increase

☐ Coverage for additional family members

☐ **Health Insurance**

Type of coverage

(If you have a high-deductible health plan, does your employer help fund a health savings account (HSA)?)

☐ **Dental and Vision**

☐ **Long-Term Care Insurance**

☐ **Education Benefits**

Benefit per semester

Conditions

☐ **Legal Benefits**

NET WORTH STATEMENT

ASSETS	AMOUNT
Primary Residence	
Second Property(s)	
Vehicles	
Boats	
Art/Jewelry/Antiques	
Cash Savings	
Money Market Savings	
CDs	
Checking/Savings	
Life Insurance	
Personal	
Group	
Mortgage	
Line of Credit	
Vacation Pay	
Retirement Savings	
Tax Deferred	
401(k)	
403(b)	
457	
SIMPLE	
SEP IRA	
Traditional IRA	
Annuities	
Tax Free	
Roth savings	
Municipal Bonds	
Brokerage Account (Nonqualified)	
Stock Options	
Mutual Funds	
Stocks	
Bonds	
Corporate	
Government	
Municipal	
Business Value	
Other	

TOTAL ASSETS

LIABILITIES	AMOUNT
Mortgage	
Other Property Mortgage(s)	
Home Equity Loan	
Personal Loan	
Education Loans	
Credit Card	
Car Loan	
Business Loan	
TOTAL LIABILITIES	
TOTAL ASSETS	
MINUS TOTAL LIABILITIES	
NET WORTH	

DIVORCE COST TRACKER

☐

☐

☐

☐

☐

☐

☐

☐

☐

☐

☐

☐

☐

☐

☐

☐

☐

☐

☐

☐

☐

☐

☐

PHASE TWO: DURING THE DIVORCE

TRANSITIONAL ACTION STEPS CHECKLIST

Do you really want your soon-to-be ex making decisions over your health or finances should you become temporarily incapacitated?

–Donna Kendrick

☐ Interview three accountant referrals, see "Interview Questions for Accountants."

☐ Interview three estate attorneys.

☐ Update your power of attorney over finances.

☐ Update your power of attorney over health care.

☐ Research healthcare provider alternatives, if needed.

☐ Determine housing costs.

☐ Complete "Should I Stay, or Should I go" worksheet.

☐ Update "Divorce Cost Tracker."

☐ Revisit your flows of income and expenses.

You have seen the income and expenses sheet in our Predivorce section, and you might be wondering why it is here again. This is your area to "noodle" different scenarios around possible financial settlements being put in front of you. Grab a pencil with a huge eraser on the end and get going. Or make a copy and title each one with a different scenario and keep going until you find equilibrium with the numbers. I really want you to have a good handle on what the costs could be to run your new life Postdivorce. Once the divorce is officially settled, you will see this worksheet again as a starting point to complete the "Should I Stay, or Should I Go" worksheet. If you have children, pay attention to future costs for their care and education, and make sure your attorney is giving you good guidance on what you can expect in the future. Basically, who pays what, and/or is it a percentage split? Since we are on the topic, please remember that 529 accounts are usually owned in one parent's name, so that parent has control over and the ability to withdraw from the account(s).

POSSIBLE FLOWS OF INCOME AND EXPENSES

Scenario Name:_____

Income

DESCRIPTION	GROSS INCOME TO DATE	OWNERSHIP	MONTHLY	ANNUAL
Employment				
Bonuses				
Investment Income				
Pensions				
Social Security				
Rental Income				
Disability Income				
Workers' Comp				
TOTAL				

Expenses

DESCRIPTION	LIABILITIES TO DATE	OWNERSHIP	MONTHLY PAYMENT	ANNUAL PAYMENT
Mortgage/Rent				
HOA Fees				
Utilities				
Phone				
Call Phone				
Internet				
Gas				
Electric				
Cable				
Trash				

Expenses

DESCRIPTION	LIABILITIES TO DATE	NECESSARY/ DISCRETIONARY	MONTHLY PAYMENT	ANNUAL PAYMENT
Sewer				
Landscaping Mov/Plow				
Food				
Groceries				
Dining Out				
Transportation				
Car Payment				
Gas				
Repairs/ Maintenance				
Tolls				
Insurance				
Child Care				
Daycare				
Babysitters				
Education Expenses				
Sport Fees				
Credit Card				

Expenses

DESCRIPTION	LIABILITIES TO DATE	NECESSARY/ DISCRETIONARY	MONTHLY PAYMENT	ANNUAL PAYMENT
Loans				
Clothing				
Dry Cleaning				
Gym Membership				
Personal Care				
Insurance Premiums				
Health				
Dental				
Eye				
Life				

Expenses

DESCRIPTION	LIABILITIES TO DATE	NECESSARY/ DISCRETIONARY	MONTHLY PAYMENT	ANNUAL PAYMENT
Disability				
Short-Term				
Long-Term				
Umbrella				
Entertainment				
Streaming				
Subscriptions				
Concerts				
Movies				
Travel				
Gifts				
Pets				
Grooming				
Vet Care				
Charitable Giving				
Other				
TOTAL				

NOTES

PHASE THREE: AFTER THE DIVORCE

POSTDIVORCE ASSET & LIABILITY INVENTORY

Primary Residence

DESCRIPTION	DATE OBTAINED	ORIGINAL VALUE	CURRENT VALUE

Secondary Properties

DESCRIPTION	DATE OBTAINED	ORIGINAL VALUE	CURRENT VALUE

Vehicles

DESCRIPTION	DATE OBTAINED	ORIGINAL VALUE	CURRENT VALUE

Boats

DESCRIPTION	DATE OBTAINED	ORIGINAL VALUE	CURRENT VALUE

Artwork/Jewelry/Antiques

DESCRIPTION	DATE OBTAINED	ORIGINAL VALUE	CURRENT VALUE

Vacation Pay

DESCRIPTION	DATE OBTAINED	CURRENT VALUE

Individual Stocks

DESCRIPTION	ACCOUNT #	COMPANY	ORIGINAL VALUE	CURRENT VALUE

Investment Brokerage Accounts

DESCRIPTION	ACCOUNT #	COMPANY	CURRENT VALUE

Bonds (Corporate, Government, Municipal)

DESCRIPTION	ACCOUNT #	COMPANY	CURRENT VALUE

Money Market Savings

DESCRIPTION	ACCOUNT #	COMPANY	CURRENT VALUE

Checking

DESCRIPTION	ACCOUNT #	COMPANY	CURRENT VALUE

Savings

DESCRIPTION	ACCOUNT #	COMPANY	CURRENT VALUE

CDs

DESCRIPTION	ACCOUNT #	DATE OF MATURITY	CURRENT VALUE	COMPANY	CURRENT VALUE

Retirement Savings in Your Name

Tax Deferred (401(k), 403(b), 457, Simple, SEP, IRA, Traditional IRA)

DESCRIPTION	ACCOUNT #	COMPANY	CURRENT VALUE

Tax Free (401(k) Roth, 403(b) Roth, 457 Roth, Simple Roth IRA, SEP IRA Roth, Roth IRA)

DESCRIPTION	ACCOUNT #	COMPANY	CURRENT VALUE

529 Plan

DESCRIPTION	ACCOUNT #	COMPANY	CURRENT VALUE

DESCRIPTION	ACCOUNT #	COMPANY	CURRENT VALUE
		W	

Trusts

DESCRIPTION	ACCOUNT #	COMPANY	CURRENT VALUE

Employer Savings and Investments

DESCRIPTION	ACCOUNT #	COMPANY	DATE OBTAINED	ORIGINAL VALUE	CURRENT VALUE

Restricted Stock Units

DESCRIPTION	ACCOUNT #	COMPANY	DATE OBTAINED	ORIGINAL VALUE	CURRENT VALUE

"SHOULD I STAY, OR SHOULD I GO?" EXERCISE ON KEEPING THE FAMILY HOME

As mentioned earlier in the story of Shirley and Larry, Shirley kept the family home in the divorce settlement. To do so, she took out a new thirty-year mortgage in her fifties and paid Larry half the home's value. Within a year of the settlement, Shirley was already struggling to make the mortgage payments. The new payment was significantly higher than before, since it was based on the equity value of the home, and interest rates had nearly doubled during the two years it took to finalize the divorce.

On top of the financial strain, Shirley found herself responsible for tasks Larry had once handled—cutting the lawn, shoveling snow, and even fixing a broken toilet flange (which she swears Larry booby-trapped before moving out). The added responsibilities limited her ability to work extra hours to increase her income.

Looking back, Shirley admitted she kept the house for emotional reasons. She wanted her children to have a familiar place to return to, though by the time the divorce was finalized, both were in college, spending summers at internships or the beach, and rarely coming home. She also confessed that she couldn't stand the thought of Larry living in the house she had worked so hard to purchase at the start of their marriage.

This story is here to help you pause, reflect, and fully consider the true impact of keeping the family home.

Can I afford our current home?

- Mortgage

- Home insurance

- State and local taxes? (School taxes can be a bugger.)

Am I physically able to maintain the property?
- If no, do I have enough money to hire someone to help me?

Emotionally, do I want to stay?

How far from work is the home?

If retired, is it time to find a new warm place to retire?

Can I keep this home and rent it out?

Do I have to make any improvements to the house?

Can I refinance and stay?

Can I qualify for a mortgage on a new home on my own?

Many times, the answer to these questions relies on how much cash you have for a down payment. You will find this answer by sitting back down with your financial professional and your plan. Withdrawals from certain investments can have big tax implications, so be sure to get professional guidance, if available. Ask: *Can I do a contingency plan? What's your threshold for a new mortgage?* I encourage you to refer to the chapter "Understanding Your Credit" and to work with a qualified mortgage broker.

How is the real estate market right now?

    Will it sell easily?

What would my capital gains be?

Can I age in place here?

Lots of steps?

Walkable area in case I can't drive?

Close to family and friends?

Big enough for my adult children to move in if care is needed?

Can I move in with them?

If I moved, where would I go?

What is average rent for home or apartment?

    Number of bedrooms needed?

    Utilities included?

    Amount first - last month's rent and security deposit?

    Additional cost of parking?

    If applicable, is it in the school district I need for the kids?

Additional thoughts:

POSTDIVORCE FLOWS OF INCOME AND EXPENSES

Income

DESCRIPTION	GROSS INCOME TO DATE	OWNERSHIP	MONTHLY	ANNUAL
Employment				
Bonuses				
Investment Income				
Pensions				
Social Security				
Rental Income				
Disability Income				
Workers' Comp				
TOTAL				

Expenses

DESCRIPTION	LIABILITIES TO DATE	NECESSARY/ DISCRETIONARY	MONTHLY PAYMENT	ANNUAL PAYMENT
Mortgage/Rent				
HOA Fees				
Utilities				
Phone				
Cell Phone				
Internet				
Gas				
Electric				
Cable				
Trash				

Expenses

DESCRIPTION	LIABILITIES TO DATE	NECESSARY/ DISCRETIONARY	MONTHLY PAYMENT	ANNUAL PAYMENT
Sewer				
Landscaping Mov/Plow				
Food				
Groceries				
Dining Out				
Transportation				
Car Payment				
Gas				
Repairs/ Maintenance				
Tolls				
Insurance				
Child Care				
Daycare				
Babysitters				
Education Expenses				
Sport Fees				
Credit Card				

Expenses

DESCRIPTION	LIABILITIES TO DATE	NECESSARY/ DISCRETIONARY	MONTHLY PAYMENT	ANNUAL PAYMENT
Loans				
Clothing				
Dry Cleaning				
Gym Membership				
Personal Care				
Insurance Premiums				
Health				
Dental				
Eye				
Life				

Expenses

DESCRIPTION	LIABILITIES TO DATE	NECESSARY/ DISCRETIONARY	MONTHLY PAYMENT	ANNUAL PAYMENT
Disability				
Short-Term				
Long-Term				
Umbrella				
Entertainment				
Streaming				
Subscriptions				
Concerts				
Movies				
Travel				
Gifts				
Pets				
Grooming				
Vet Care				
Charitable Giving				
Other				
TOTAL				

Yearly Summary

DESCRIPTION	MONTHLY	ANNUAL
Total Income		
Necessary Expenses		
Discretionary Expenses		
Overage/Underage		

NOTES

NOTES

POSTDIVORCE BENEFITS INVENTORY

Salary

Frequency of pay

☐ Biweekly

☐ Every other week

☐ Once a month

Commission or Bonuses?

Pay Increases

☐ Guaranteed

☐ Merit or cost of living

☐ At review or annual?

☐ Nonqualified deferred compensation

These are benefits you may lose should you leave the employer. Many times, they are stock incentives for highly compensated employees to "make them sticky" to the job. (i.e., if they leave the company, they are leaving money on the table.)

Ability To Promote Upward

☐ Ask for your company's organizational chart.

Work Schedule

☐ Telecommuting?

☐ Flexible Hours? Core Hours?

☐ Mandatory Overtime?

☐ Travel?

Benefits

☐ **Short-Term Disability**

Waiting period

Percentage of coverage

☐ **Long-Term Disability**

Waiting period

Percentage of coverage

Maximum benefit

☐ **Life Insurance**

☐ Ability to increase

☐ Coverage for additional family members

☐ **Health Insurance**

Type of coverage

(If you have a high-deductible health plan, does your employer help fund a health savings account (HSA)?)

☐ **Dental and Vision**

☐ **Long-term Care Insurance**

☐ **Education Benefits**

Benefit per semester

Conditions

☐ **Legal Benefits**

POSTDIVORCE NET WORTH STATEMENT

ASSETS	AMOUNT
Primary Residence	
Second Property(s)	
Vehicles	
Boats	
Art/Jewelry/Antiques	
Cash Savings	
Money Market Savings	
CDs	
Checking/Savings	
Life Insurance	
Personal	
Group	
Mortgage	
Line of Credit	
Vacation Pay	
Retirement Savings	
Tax Deferred	
401(k)	
403(b)	
457	
SIMPLE	
SEP IRA	
Traditional IRA	
Annuities	
Tax Free	
Roth savings	
Municipal Bonds	

Brokerage Account (Nonqualified)	
Stock Options	
Mutual Funds	
Stocks	
Bonds	
Corporate	
Government	
Municipal	
Business Value	
Other	

TOTAL ASSETS

LIABILITIES	AMOUNT
Mortgage	
Other Property Mortgage(s)	
Home Equity Loan	
Personal Loan	
Education Loans	
Credit Card	
Car Loan	
Business Loan	
TOTAL LIABILITIES	
TOTAL ASSETS	
MINUS TOTAL LIABILITIES	
NET WORTH	

POSTDIVORCE ACTION STEPS CHECKLIST

- ☐ Real Estate Title/Deeds
- ☐ Loans
- ☐ Mortgages
- ☐ Vehicles

Investments
- ☐ 401(k), 403(b), etc.
- ☐ IRAs
- ☐ Pension Funds
- ☐ Brokerage/Taxable Accounts

Bank Accounts
- ☐ Safe-Deposit Boxes

Insurance Policies
- ☐ Auto
- ☐ Home
- ☐ Umbrella
- ☐ Life

- ☐ Run your credit report, ninety days postdivorce **www.annualcreditreport.com.**

- ☐ Complete your Postdivorce Asset & Liability Inventory, page 118.
- ☐ Complete your Postdivorce Flows of Income, page.
- ☐ Complete/Update your Postdivorce Personal Document Locator.
- ☐ Create your new financial plan with your CFP®.
- ☐ Create your new estate documents.
  - ☐ Wills and Trusts
  - ☐ POA over Finance
  - ☐ POA over Health Care
  - ☐ POA over Digital Assets
  - ☐ Health Care Directive

Inform the human resources of your company of your new marital status.
- ☐ Update tax filing status.
- ☐ Update any withholding amounts (Consult your accountant for additional guidance.)

Update any changes to health insurance with your carrier.
- ☐ Remove your ex-spouse from medical information sharing and HIPAA authorizations.
- ☐ Update school administrators and counselors on the new contact information and email address for school-related matters.

SUPPORT SYSTEMS & PLANNING AHEAD

HEALTH INSURANCE

Often in divorce, one party has the health insurance coverage, and the other will be removed from that shared coverage once the divorce is settled. In the past, many couples would stay married simply for the health-care coverage, possibly living apart and acting as single, but on paper, married filing jointly for taxes to keep health-care coverage from the employer.

I want more for you, my new friend. I want you to be free to live your best life now that this relationship has matured to a new form, understanding how we obtain health coverage, the costs, and how those costs are determined. Use that information to make educated choices during negotiations and the acceptance of a settlement.

Health Insurance Made Simple

Let's face it—in today's world, health insurance is a necessity. In fact, most US. citizens and legal residents must have qualifying health insurance or face a penalty tax. Yet the cost of medical care is soaring higher every year, and it's becoming increasingly difficult (and in some cases, impossible) to pay medical costs out of pocket. Whether you already have health insurance or want to get it, here's some basic information to help you understand it.

Not Part of a Group? You May Have to Go It Alone

You may have group health insurance or be able to buy it through your employer. Group insurance is most commonly offered through employers. It is also offered through some civic groups and other organizations (e.g., auto clubs, chambers of commerce). A single policy covers the medical expenses of a group of people. All eligible members of the group can be covered by a group policy regardless of age or physical condition. The premium for group insurance is calculated based on characteristics of the group as a whole, such as average age and degree of occupational hazard. It's generally less expensive than individual insurance.

If you can't join a group, consider buying individual insurance. Unlike group insurance, individual insurance is purchased directly from an insurance company or agent. When you apply, you are evaluated in terms of how much risk you present to the insurance company. Your risk potential will determine whether you qualify for insurance and how much it will cost, depending on state laws. You must pay the full premiums yourself. If you have to go it alone, you can shop for health insurance coverage through state-based Affordable Insurance Marketplaces.

You can compare health plans according to price and quality and ultimately purchase an affordable plan that best meets your health insurance needs.

Know What's Out There

The cost and range of protection that your health insurance provides will depend on your insurance provider and the particular policy you purchase. You may have comprehensive health insurance that involves several types of coverage, or basic coverage that includes hospital, surgical, and physicians' expenses. In addition, major medical coverage is necessary in the event of a catastrophic accident or illness. Many plans also cover prescriptions, mental health services, and other health-related activities (e.g., health club memberships).

When it comes to health insurance, HMO, PPO, and POS are more than just letters. You need to know the types of health plans available so that you can make an informed decision. You can obtain health insurance through traditional insurers, such as Blue Cross/Blue Shield, health maintenance organizations (HMOs), preferred provider organizations (PPOs), point of service (POS) plans, and exclusive provider organizations (EPOs).

- **Traditional insurers:** These plans usually allow you flexibility regarding choice of doctors and other health-care providers. Some policies reimburse you for covered expenses, while others make payments directly to medical providers. You will pay a deductible and a percentage of each bill, known as coinsurance.
- **HMOs:** Health maintenance organizations cover only medical treatment provided by physicians and facilities within their networks. You must choose a primary care physician, who will either approve or deny any requests to see a specialist. You usually pay a fixed monthly fee for health-care coverage, as well as small co-payments (e.g., $10 for each office visit and prescription).
- **PPOs:** Preferred provider organizations do not require members to seek care from PPO physicians and hospitals, but there is usually a strong financial incentive to do so (in terms of percentage of reimbursement). You usually pay a fixed monthly fee for health-care coverage, as well as small co-payments (e.g., $10 for each office visit and prescription).
- **POSs:** Point of service plans combine characteristics of the HMO and PPO. You must choose a primary care physician to be responsible for all of your referrals within the POS network. Although you can choose to go outside the network with this type of plan, your health care will be covered at a lower level.
- **EPOs:** Exclusive provider organizations are basically PPOs with one important difference: EPOs provide no coverage for non-network care.

Read Your Contract

You should have a basic understanding of what your policy does and does not cover. This may help you prevent an unexpected medical bill from arriving in your mailbox, because you'll know ahead of time, for instance, whether or not liposuction is covered.

You must read your policy carefully, particularly the section on limitations and exclusions. The specifics will vary from policy to policy. In general, though, most policies will at least mention the following:

- **Pre-existing conditions:** An illness or injury that began or occurred before you obtained coverage under the policy. The Affordable Care Act eliminated the ability of health insurance policies or plans to deny coverage for pre-existing conditions that cover essential health benefits. However, pre-existing conditions may be excluded for non essential health benefits.
- **Nonduplication of benefits:** Benefits will not be paid for amounts reimbursed by other insurance companies.

Your health insurance policy should also address the following issues:

- **Deductible:** The amount that you must pay before insurance coverage begins (usually an annual figure).
- **Coinsurance:** The portion of each medical bill for which you are responsible.
- **Co-payment:** The fixed fee that you pay for each doctor visit or prescription.
- **Family coverage:** Many group plans allow you to cover your spouse and dependents for an increased premium.
- **Out-of-pocket maximum:** This provision is designed to limit your liability for medical expenses in the calendar year; you won't have to make coinsurance payments in excess of this figure.
- **Benefit ceiling:** The maximum lifetime payout under the insurance policy, usually at least one million dollars.

LOWERING THE COST OF HEALTH CARE

America's spending on health care is growing faster than the rest of the economy. What are the reasons for this, and what can you do to lower your health-care costs?

Why Is the Cost of Health Insurance Rising?

The primary reason for premium increases is the rising cost of health care itself. Several factors are contributing to the rise in health care costs:

- Increase in the average age of the population.
- New medical technology.
- High administrative costs.
- More government regulation.
- Oversupply of health-care facilities.
- Overuse and misuse of medical services.
- Prescription price increases and their increased use.
- Tougher medical provider negotiations with health plans.
- Consumer demands for easier and broader access to care.
- The medical needs and demands of seventy-seven million baby boomers.
- Investors putting pressure on insurance companies to be profitable.

What can you do to lower the cost of health insurance? Obviously, there are areas you have no control over. But there are some things you can do.

Become an Informed Consumer

Group insurance is less expensive than individual health insurance. If you can't get group coverage from your employer, investigate buying insurance through another group, such as a fraternal or professional association.

If individual coverage is the only alternative, look at different types of plans. For example, if you need insurance for you and your spouse, individual policies may be less expensive than a family plan. Research the benefits and options. Find out which best suit you and your family. Don't buy more insurance than you need. Many online resources are available to help you purchase health insurance. However, an insurance agent or financial advisor may save you both time and money.

You may be able to save money by self-insuring against routine medical expenses (i.e., paying routine medical expenses out of pocket) and buying major medical insurance to cover only costly illnesses or emergencies. If your cash reserve is large enough to cover minor medical expenses, you may want to consider choosing a higher deductible. For example, increasing your deductible from $250 to $500 could significantly lower your insurance premiums.

You may also shop for health insurance coverage through either a state-based or the federal health insurance Marketplace. You can compare health plans according to price and quality and purchase an affordable plan through a Marketplace that best meets your health insurance needs.

Other Ways to Reduce Premiums

- Avoid purchasing single-disease policies.
- Avoid duplicating any coverage your spouse may have from his or her employer.
- Ask how much you can save by paying premiums annually.

After you determine what you need, compare at least three companies for the best deal. Remember that the lowest price does not necessarily mean the best plan. Ask questions such as:

- What is the plan's history of premium increases?
- How much notice is given before a premium increase?
- How are deductible and out-of-pocket costs figured?
- What are the co-payment levels, and when are they charged? What is excluded?
- How long is the free-look period?
- Is the insurance company financially healthy?

Try to get quality and accreditation reports on the plans you are considering. Quality reports contain consumer ratings that outline how satisfied consumers are with the doctors in their plan and how well a health-care organization prevents and treats illnesses. Accreditation reports give information on how accredited organizations meet national standards and often include clinical performance measures. Most employer groups can provide this information. Talk to your plan's administrator or customer service department.

Be Truthful

Be truthful on the insurance application. If you make a minor error, such as your month of birth, there shouldn't be a problem. However, if you fail to report that you are a smoker, benefits could be denied for smoker-related problems that you might later develop. Worse yet, your policy could be rescinded, leaving you with no coverage at all.

Control Your Out-of-Pocket Expenses

Avoid unnecessary surgery. Ask questions. If it's not an emergency, find out if there are alternative treatments. It is your responsibility to make sure that you are covered for certain procedures. If you choose an elective surgery, make sure that your policy will cover it. Do the benefits include hospital and doctor's fees? Some plans pay only one or the other.

Does the plan pay a percentage of the actual costs, or does it pay based on a set fee schedule? A plan that pays 80 percent of a fee schedule instead of 80 percent of the actual costs can end up costing you more out of pocket. Ask your doctor if he or she will agree to accept the insurance company's set fee. And ask about home health care for your recovery. Home care would be less expensive than a nursing home or hospital stay, and you'd be able to recover in the more comfortable environment of your own home.

Take Advantage of Tax Deductions

Medical expenses are generally deductible to the extent that they exceed 7.5 percent of your adjusted gross income. Deductible expenses can include:

- Insurance premiums
- Prescriptions
- Doctors and dentists
- Hospitals and clinics
- Lab and x-ray fees
- Glasses and contact lenses
- Transportation for medical reasons

Work to Continually Save Money

- Live a healthy lifestyle. For example, a smoker who quits can usually receive a premium reduction.
- Ask your insurance company about other discounts.
- Take advantage of free health screenings at local clinics, hospitals, and health fairs. Avoid the overuse of antibiotics.
- Watch your co-payments and out-of-pocket expenses to make sure that you don't overpay.

Each year, check the coverage of your policy. Ensure that it's keeping pace with the evolving needs of you and your family. Check rates when your lifestyle changes, such as moving to a new part of the country or getting married. When your children go off to college, look into college health plans. Some are subsidized by tuition and might save you money.

Reducing the amount of care you require will pay off. You will save money in out-of-pocket costs, insurance premiums, and lost time from work. But the greatest payoff will be a longer and healthier life.

HEALTH INSURANCE AND COBRA

If you're like most Americans, you count on your employer for health insurance coverage. But what would happen to your health insurance if you suddenly stopped working or no longer qualified for benefits? No one can predict the future. It's possible that your company could lay you off or reduce your hours to part-time, your spouse could die, or your marriage could end in divorce. If something unexpected happened, you could be left without health benefits. And remember, buying private health insurance on your own can be pretty costly, especially if you're out of work.

Fortunately, there's the Consolidated Omnibus Budget Reconciliation Act of 1986 (COBRA). COBRA can prove to be a real lifesaver for you and your family when your health coverage is jeopardized. You may also benefit from the Health Insurance Portability and Accountability Act of 1996 (HIPAA), which took some further steps toward health-care reform.

COBRA Explained

COBRA is a federal law designed to protect employees and their dependents from losing health insurance coverage as a result of job loss or divorce. If you and your dependents are covered by an employer-sponsored health insurance plan, a provision of COBRA entitles you to continue coverage when you'd normally lose it. Most larger employers (those with twenty or more employees) are required to offer COBRA coverage.

As an employee, you're entitled to COBRA coverage only if your employment has been terminated for any reason other than gross misconduct or if your hours have been reduced. However, your spouse and dependent children may be eligible for COBRA benefits if they're no longer entitled to employer-sponsored benefits because of divorce, death, or certain other events.

Unfortunately, you can't continue your health insurance coverage forever. You may be able to continue your health insurance under COBRA for a certain time period (pleases reference your State's guidelines) if your employment has been terminated, if your hours have been reduced, or other qualifying reasons.

- **Divorce:** If your former spouse maintained family health coverage through work (and works for a company with a least twenty employees), you may be able to continue this group coverage for a period of time after the divorce or legal separation (each State is different, so take the time to reference the appropriate State specific guidance). You'll have to pay for this coverage, though. Your cost of continuing coverage cannot exceed 102 percent of the employer's cost for insurance. COBRA coverage many change if you remarry or obtain coverage under another group health plan.
- **Company goes out of business:** Unfortunately, you may be out of luck here. If your company goes out of business and no longer has a group health insurance policy in force, then COBRA coverage will not be available. (A possible exception involves union employees covered by a collective bargaining agreement.)

COBRA Expanded

In 1996, HIPAA expanded certain COBRA provisions and created other health-care rights. In many ways, HIPAA took a significant step toward health-care reform in the United States.

Some of its provisions may affect you. The major provisions of HIPAA:

- Allow workers to move from one employer to another without fear of losing group health insurance.
- Require health insurance companies that serve small groups (two to fifty employees) to accept every small employer that applies for coverage.
- Increase the tax deductibility of medical insurance premiums for the self-employed.
- Require health insurance plans to provide inpatient coverage for a mother and newborn infant for at least forty-eight hours after a normal birth or ninety-six hours after a cesarean section.

For example, assume you're pregnant and covered by a group health insurance plan at work. You decide to take a job at another firm. Under HIPAA, pregnancy cannot be considered a pre-existing condition for a woman who's changing jobs if she was previously covered by a group health insurance plan. So, if you had insurance at your old job, you can't be denied health insurance coverage at your new job simply because you're pregnant.

However, many companies require you to be employed for thirty days or more before you become eligible for coverage. If you are nearing the end of your pregnancy, and that requirement poses a problem for you, you may be eligible for coverage under COBRA through your former employer.

FINANCIAL PLANNING: HELPING YOU SEE THE BIG PICTURE

Do you picture yourself owning a new home, starting a business, or retiring comfortably? These are a few of the financial goals that may be important to you, and each comes with a price tag attached. That's where financial planning comes in. Financial planning is a process that can help you target your goals by evaluating your whole financial picture, then outlining strategies that are tailored to your individual needs and available resources.

Why Financial Planning Is Important

A comprehensive financial plan serves as a framework for organizing the pieces of your financial picture. With a financial plan in place, you'll be better able to focus on your goals and understand what it will take to reach them. One of the main benefits of having a financial plan is that it can help you balance competing financial priorities. A financial plan will clearly show you how your financial goals are related—for example, how saving for your children's college education might impact your ability to save for retirement. Then you can use the information you've gleaned to decide how to prioritize your goals, implement specific strategies, and choose suitable products or services. Best of all, you'll know that your financial life is headed in the right direction.

The Financial Planning Process

Creating and implementing a comprehensive financial plan generally involves working with financial professionals to:

- Develop a clear picture of your current financial situation by reviewing your income, assets, and liabilities, and evaluating your insurance coverage, your investment portfolio, your tax exposure, and your estate plan.
- Establish and prioritize financial goals and time frames for achieving these goals.
- Implement strategies that address your current financial weaknesses and build on your financial strengths.
- Choose specific products and services that are tailored to help meet your financial objectives.*
- Monitor your plan, making adjustments as your goals, time frames, or circumstances change

There is no assurance that working with a financial professional will improve investment results.

Common Financial Goals

- Saving and investing for retirement.
- Saving and investing for college.
- Establishing an emergency fund.
- Providing for your family in the event of your death.
- Minimizing income or estate taxes.

Some Members of the Team

The financial planning process can involve a number of professionals.

- Financial planners typically play a central role in the process, focusing on your overall financial plan and often coordinating the activities of other professionals who have expertise in specific areas.
- Accountants or tax attorneys provide advice on federal and state tax issues.
- Estate planning attorneys help you plan your estate and give advice on transferring and managing your assets before and after your death.
- Insurance professionals evaluate insurance needs and recommend appropriate products and strategies.
- Investment advisors provide advice about investment options and asset allocation and can help you plan a strategy to manage your investment portfolio.

The most important member of the team, however, is you. Your needs and objectives drive the team, and once you've carefully considered any recommendations, all decisions lie in your hands.

Why Can't I do It Myself?

You can, if you have enough time and knowledge, but developing a comprehensive financial plan may require expertise in several areas. A financial professional can give you objective information and help you weigh your alternatives, saving you time and ensuring that all angles of your financial picture are covered.

Staying On Track

The financial planning process doesn't end once your initial plan has been created. Your plan should generally be reviewed at least once a year to make sure that it's up-to-date. It's also possible that you'll need to modify your plan due to changes in your personal circumstances or the economy. Here are some of the events that might trigger a review of your financial plan:

- Your goals or time horizons change.
- You experience a life-changing event such as marriage, the birth of a child, health problems, or a job loss.
- You have a specific or immediate financial planning need (e.g., drafting a will, managing a distribution from a retirement account, paying long-term care expenses).
- Your income or expenses substantially increase or decrease.
- Your portfolio hasn't performed as expected.
- You're affected by changes to the economy or tax laws.

Financial Planning Frequently Asked Questions

Q: What if I'm too busy?

A: Don't wait until you're in the midst of a financial crisis before beginning the planning process. The sooner you start, the more options you may have.

Q: Is the financial planning process complicated?

A: Each financial plan is tailored to the needs of the individual, so how complicated the process will be depends on your individual circumstances. But no matter what type of help you need, a financial professional will work hard to make the process as easy as possible and will gladly answer all of your questions.

Q: Can I still control my own finances?

A: A financial planner can help guide you in your decisions. You retain control over your finances. Recommendations will be based on your needs, values, goals, and time frames. You decide which recommendations to follow, then work with a financial professional to implement them.

FINAL THOUGHTS

If you've reached this page, you most likely are divorced or waiting for the judge to stamp your final decree. If you completed the pages of this workbook, you are now at the point where you understand what assets are in your name as well as what moves are needed in the future to fulfill your settlement. For many, this is a time to feel relief. If you were a child of the '70s, like me, there was a famous commercial for an antacid whose tag line was, "How do you spell relief?" After my parents' divorce, my dad used to chime in over the commercial: "How does Phil spell relief? D-I-V O-R-C-E."

All joking aside, for many, post-divorce is not a time of relief, but a time of frustration because the life they envisioned is no longer. Often, the lifestyle they lived before divorce has been compromised, altered, or degraded. I beg of you to have hope and to give this some time. It may take a year to adjust to this new way of living, and then you can assess your spending plan, determine what you can afford, and consider what changes you might want to make in year two.

In year three, you might be ready to buy a home, move to a new town, or find new love. No matter what side of the fence you are on, I highly encourage you to reconnect with your financial planner at this point (you found a good one predivorce, right? If not, circle back to "Financial Advisor Interview Questions", my angel.)

At this point, you can share the postdivorce workbook pages with your advisor and create a financial plan for the immediate days ahead. Create savings or spending goals for the next few years. Many of us seek answers to questions like, "Am I going to be okay?" and long-term financial planning provides truly valuable guidance so you can know that you will be more than okay. You will have clarity on the answers to "Do I have to save more? Spend less? Or work longer?" Identify what your long-term might look like. Maybe even dream a little. Once you have this new road map, you are in control, my friend.

Keep going. I'm proud of you.

DREAMING PAGES/LONG-TERM PLANNING

Lifelong Dreamy Goals:

If you live to 100 years old, what would your obituary say?

NOTES

MY 10-YEAR GOALS:

Personal:

Community:

Career:

Mission:

MY 5-YEAR GOALS:

Personal:

Community:

Career:

Mission:

MY 3-YEAR GOALS:

Personal:

_____

_____

_____

_____

_____

_____

Community:

_____

_____

_____

_____

_____

_____

Career:

_____

_____

_____

_____

_____

_____

Mission:

_____

_____

_____

_____

_____

_____

MY 1-YEAR GOALS:

Personal:

Community:

Career:

Mission:

MY FOCUS FOR THE NEXT 90 DAYS:

Personal:

Community:

Career:

Mission:

MY FOCUS FOR THE NEXT 30 DAYS:

Personal:

Community:

Career:

Mission:

EXTRAS & RESOURCES

RESOURCE DIRECTORY

The resources listed here are provided for your convenience and information. They are presented in no particular order. Inclusion on this list does not constitute an endorsement, recommendation, or guarantee of any product, service, or organization. Please use your own judgment when selecting and engaging with any of these resources.

CERTIFIED FINANCIAL PLANNERS®:
https://www.letsmakeaplan.org/find-a-cfp-professional

Certified Divorce Financial Analysts:
https://institutedfa.com/

Certified Public Accountants:
https://nasba.org/features/nasbalaunchescpaverify/

IRS Directory of Federal Tax Return Preparers:
https://irs.treasury.gov/rpo/rpo.jsf

American Bar Association–Find Legal Help:
https://www.americanbar.org/groups/legal_services/flh-home/

Bar Association Directory:
https://www.barassociationdirectory.com/

National Association of Divorce Professionals:
https://thenadp.com/search-members/

Academy of Professional Family Mediators (APFM):
https://apfmnet.org/

National Association of Certified Mediators (NACM):
https://www.mediatorcertification.org/

Association for Conflict Resolution (ACR):
https://acrnet.org/

International Academy of Collaborative Professionals (IACP):
https://www.collaborativepractice.com/

Certified Divorce Coaches:
https://certifieddivorcecoach.com/find-a-divorce-coach-2/

Licensed Marriage, Family and Life Therapists:

- https://www.psychologytoday.com/us/therapists
- https://www.goodtherapy.org/
- https://www.betterhelp.com/

CALENDAR

_____ _____
MONTH   YEAR

Monday_____**through Sunday**_____
              DATE   DATE

MONDAY	TUESDAY

WEDNESDAY	THURSDAY

FRIDAY	SATURDAY	SUNDAY

NOTES/CONVERSATIONS

CALENDAR

_____ _____
MONTH   YEAR

Monday_____through Sunday_____
DATE   DATE

MONDAY	TUESDAY

WEDNESDAY	THURSDAY

FRIDAY	SATURDAY	SUNDAY

NOTES/CONVERSATIONS

_____ _____
MONTH   YEAR

Monday_____through Sunday_____

DATE   DATE

MONDAY	TUESDAY

WEDNESDAY	THURSDAY

FRIDAY	SATURDAY	SUNDAY

CALENDAR

_____ _____
MONTH   YEAR

Monday_____**through Sunday**_____
DATE   DATE

MONDAY	TUESDAY

WEDNESDAY	THURSDAY

FRIDAY	SATURDAY	SUNDAY

NOTES/CONVERSATIONS

_____ _____
MONTH   YEAR

Monday_____**through Sunday**_____
DATE   DATE

MONDAY	TUESDAY

WEDNESDAY	THURSDAY

FRIDAY	SATURDAY	SUNDAY

NOTES/CONVERSATIONS

CALENDAR

_____   _____

MONTH   YEAR

Monday_____through Sunday_____
DATE   DATE

MONDAY	TUESDAY

WEDNESDAY	THURSDAY

FRIDAY	SATURDAY	SUNDAY

NOTES/CONVERSATIONS

CALENDAR

_____ _____
MONTH   YEAR

Monday_____through Sunday_____

DATE   DATE

MONDAY	TUESDAY

WEDNESDAY	THURSDAY

FRIDAY	SATURDAY	SUNDAY

NOTES/CONVERSATIONS

CALENDAR

_____ _____
MONTH   YEAR

Monday_____through Sunday_____
DATE   DATE

MONDAY	TUESDAY

WEDNESDAY	THURSDAY

FRIDAY	SATURDAY	SUNDAY

NOTES/CONVERSATIONS

CALENDAR

_____ _____
MONTH   YEAR

Monday_____through Sunday_____
DATE   DATE

MONDAY	TUESDAY

WEDNESDAY	THURSDAY

FRIDAY	SATURDAY	SUNDAY

NOTES/CONVERSATIONS

CALENDAR

_____ _____
MONTH   YEAR

Monday_____through Sunday_____
DATE   DATE

MONDAY	TUESDAY

WEDNESDAY	THURSDAY

FRIDAY	SATURDAY	SUNDAY

NOTES/CONVERSATIONS

CALENDAR

_____ _____
MONTH   YEAR

Monday_____through Sunday_____
DATE   DATE

MONDAY	TUESDAY

WEDNESDAY	THURSDAY

FRIDAY	SATURDAY	SUNDAY

NOTES/CONVERSATIONS

CALENDAR

Monday_____through Sunday_____

DATE   DATE

MONDAY	TUESDAY

WEDNESDAY	THURSDAY

FRIDAY	SATURDAY	SUNDAY

NOTES/CONVERSATIONS

CALENDAR

_____   _____
MONTH   YEAR

Monday_____through Sunday_____
DATE   DATE

MONDAY	TUESDAY

WEDNESDAY	THURSDAY

FRIDAY	SATURDAY	SUNDAY

NOTES/CONVERSATIONS

CALENDAR

_____   _____
MONTH   YEAR

Monday_____through Sunday_____
DATE   DATE

MONDAY	TUESDAY

WEDNESDAY	THURSDAY

FRIDAY	SATURDAY	SUNDAY

NOTES/CONVERSATIONS

CALENDAR

_____ MONTH _____ YEAR

Monday_____**through Sunday**_____
DATE   DATE

MONDAY	TUESDAY

WEDNESDAY	THURSDAY

FRIDAY	SATURDAY	SUNDAY

NOTES/CONVERSATIONS

CALENDAR

_____ _____
MONTH   YEAR

Monday_____through Sunday_____
DATE   DATE

MONDAY	TUESDAY

WEDNESDAY	THURSDAY

FRIDAY	SATURDAY	SUNDAY

NOTES/CONVERSATIONS

CALENDAR

_____   _____
MONTH   YEAR

Monday_____through Sunday_____
DATE   DATE

MONDAY	TUESDAY

WEDNESDAY	THURSDAY

FRIDAY	SATURDAY	SUNDAY

NOTES/CONVERSATIONS

CALENDAR

_____ _____
MONTH   YEAR

Monday_____through Sunday_____
DATE   DATE

MONDAY	TUESDAY

WEDNESDAY	THURSDAY

FRIDAY	SATURDAY	SUNDAY

CALENDAR

_____ _____
MONTH   YEAR

Monday_____through Sunday_____
DATE   DATE

MONDAY	TUESDAY

WEDNESDAY	THURSDAY

FRIDAY	SATURDAY	SUNDAY

NOTES/CONVERSATIONS

CALENDAR

_____   _____
MONTH   YEAR

Monday_____**through Sunday**_____
DATE   DATE

MONDAY	TUESDAY

WEDNESDAY	THURSDAY

FRIDAY	SATURDAY	SUNDAY

NOTES/CONVERSATIONS

CALENDAR

_____   _____
MONTH   YEAR

Monday_____through Sunday_____
DATE   DATE

MONDAY	TUESDAY

WEDNESDAY	THURSDAY

FRIDAY	SATURDAY	SUNDAY

NOTES/CONVERSATIONS

CALENDAR

_____ _____
MONTH   YEAR

Monday_____through Sunday_____
DATE   DATE

MONDAY	TUESDAY

WEDNESDAY	THURSDAY

FRIDAY	SATURDAY	SUNDAY

NOTES/CONVERSATIONS

CALENDAR

_____ _____
MONTH   YEAR

Monday_____**through Sunday**_____
            DATE   DATE

MONDAY	TUESDAY

WEDNESDAY	THURSDAY

FRIDAY	SATURDAY	SUNDAY

NOTES/CONVERSATIONS

CALENDAR

Monday_____**through Sunday**_____
DATE   DATE

MONDAY	TUESDAY

WEDNESDAY	THURSDAY

FRIDAY	SATURDAY	SUNDAY

NOTES/CONVERSATIONS

CALENDAR

_____   _____
MONTH   YEAR

Monday_____through Sunday_____
         DATE   DATE

MONDAY	TUESDAY

WEDNESDAY	THURSDAY

FRIDAY	SATURDAY	SUNDAY

NOTES/CONVERSATIONS

CALENDAR

_____ _____
MONTH   YEAR

Monday_____**through Sunday**_____
DATE   DATE

MONDAY	TUESDAY

WEDNESDAY	THURSDAY

FRIDAY	SATURDAY	SUNDAY

NOTES/CONVERSATIONS

CALENDAR

_____ _____
MONTH   YEAR

Monday_____through Sunday_____
DATE   DATE

MONDAY	TUESDAY

WEDNESDAY	THURSDAY

FRIDAY	SATURDAY	SUNDAY

NOTES/CONVERSATIONS

CALENDAR

_____ _____
MONTH   YEAR

Monday_____through Sunday_____
DATE   DATE

MONDAY	TUESDAY

WEDNESDAY	THURSDAY

FRIDAY	SATURDAY	SUNDAY

NOTES/CONVERSATIONS

CALENDAR

_____ _____
MONTH   YEAR

Monday_____through Sunday_____
DATE   DATE

MONDAY	TUESDAY

WEDNESDAY	THURSDAY

FRIDAY	SATURDAY	SUNDAY

NOTES/CONVERSATIONS

CALENDAR

_____ _____
MONTH   YEAR

Monday_____through Sunday_____
DATE   DATE

MONDAY	TUESDAY

WEDNESDAY	THURSDAY

FRIDAY	SATURDAY	SUNDAY

CALENDAR

_____   _____
MONTH   YEAR

Monday_____through Sunday_____
DATE   DATE

MONDAY	TUESDAY

WEDNESDAY	THURSDAY

FRIDAY	SATURDAY	SUNDAY

NOTES/CONVERSATIONS

CALENDAR

_____ _____
MONTH   YEAR

Monday_____through Sunday_____

DATE   DATE

MONDAY	TUESDAY

WEDNESDAY	THURSDAY

FRIDAY	SATURDAY	SUNDAY

NOTES/CONVERSATIONS

CALENDAR

————————— —————————
MONTH   YEAR

Monday————**through Sunday**————
DATE   DATE

MONDAY	TUESDAY

WEDNESDAY	THURSDAY

FRIDAY	SATURDAY	SUNDAY

NOTES/CONVERSATIONS

CALENDAR

_____ _____
MONTH   YEAR

Monday_____through Sunday_____
DATE   DATE

MONDAY	TUESDAY

WEDNESDAY	THURSDAY

FRIDAY	SATURDAY	SUNDAY

NOTES/CONVERSATIONS

CALENDAR

_____   _____
MONTH   YEAR

Monday_____through Sunday_____
DATE   DATE

MONDAY	TUESDAY

WEDNESDAY	THURSDAY

FRIDAY	SATURDAY	SUNDAY

NOTES/CONVERSATIONS

CALENDAR

MONTH   YEAR

Monday_____**through Sunday**_____

DATE   DATE

MONDAY	TUESDAY

WEDNESDAY	THURSDAY

FRIDAY	SATURDAY	SUNDAY

NOTES/CONVERSATIONS

CALENDAR

_____ _____
MONTH   YEAR

Monday_____through Sunday_____
DATE   DATE

MONDAY	TUESDAY

WEDNESDAY	THURSDAY

FRIDAY	SATURDAY	SUNDAY

NOTES/CONVERSATIONS

CALENDAR

_____ _____
MONTH   YEAR

Monday_____**through Sunday**_____
        DATE   DATE

MONDAY	TUESDAY

WEDNESDAY	THURSDAY

FRIDAY	SATURDAY	SUNDAY

NOTES/CONVERSATIONS

CALENDAR

_____ _____
MONTH   YEAR

Monday_____through Sunday_____
DATE   DATE

MONDAY	TUESDAY

WEDNESDAY	THURSDAY

FRIDAY	SATURDAY	SUNDAY

NOTES/CONVERSATIONS

CALENDAR

_____ _____
MONTH   YEAR

Monday_____through Sunday_____
DATE   DATE

MONDAY	TUESDAY

WEDNESDAY	THURSDAY

FRIDAY	SATURDAY	SUNDAY

CALENDAR

_____ _____
MONTH   YEAR

Monday_____through Sunday_____
DATE   DATE

MONDAY	TUESDAY

WEDNESDAY	THURSDAY

FRIDAY	SATURDAY	SUNDAY

NOTES/CONVERSATIONS

CALENDAR

_____   _____
MONTH   YEAR

Monday_____through Sunday_____
DATE   DATE

MONDAY	TUESDAY

WEDNESDAY	THURSDAY

FRIDAY	SATURDAY	SUNDAY

NOTES/CONVERSATIONS

CALENDAR

_____   _____
MONTH   YEAR

Monday_____through Sunday_____
DATE   DATE

MONDAY	TUESDAY

WEDNESDAY	THURSDAY

FRIDAY	SATURDAY	SUNDAY

NOTES/CONVERSATIONS

CALENDAR

_____ _____
MONTH   YEAR

Monday_____through Sunday_____

DATE   DATE

MONDAY	TUESDAY

WEDNESDAY	THURSDAY

FRIDAY	SATURDAY	SUNDAY

NOTES/CONVERSATIONS

CALENDAR

_____   _____
MONTH   YEAR

Monday_____through Sunday_____
DATE   DATE

MONDAY	TUESDAY

WEDNESDAY	THURSDAY

FRIDAY	SATURDAY	SUNDAY

NOTES/CONVERSATIONS

CALENDAR

_____   _____
MONTH   YEAR

Monday_____through Sunday_____
DATE   DATE

MONDAY	TUESDAY

WEDNESDAY	THURSDAY

FRIDAY	SATURDAY	SUNDAY

NOTES/CONVERSATIONS

_____ _____
MONTH   YEAR

Monday_____through Sunday_____
DATE   DATE

MONDAY	TUESDAY

WEDNESDAY	THURSDAY

FRIDAY	SATURDAY	SUNDAY

NOTES/CONVERSATIONS

CALENDAR

_____ _____
MONTH YEAR

Monday_____**through Sunday**_____
DATE DATE

MONDAY	TUESDAY

WEDNESDAY	THURSDAY

FRIDAY	SATURDAY	SUNDAY

NOTES/CONVERSATIONS

CALENDAR

_____ _____
MONTH   YEAR

Monday_____through Sunday_____
DATE   DATE

MONDAY	TUESDAY

WEDNESDAY	THURSDAY

FRIDAY	SATURDAY	SUNDAY

NOTES/CONVERSATIONS

CALENDAR

_____ _____
MONTH   YEAR

Monday_____through Sunday_____
        DATE   DATE

MONDAY	TUESDAY

WEDNESDAY	THURSDAY

FRIDAY	SATURDAY	SUNDAY

NOTES/CONVERSATIONS

_____ _____
MONTH   YEAR

Monday_____through Sunday_____
DATE   DATE

MONDAY	TUESDAY

WEDNESDAY	THURSDAY

FRIDAY	SATURDAY	SUNDAY

NOTES/CONVERSATIONS

CALENDAR

MONTH   YEAR

Monday_____**through Sunday**_____

DATE   DATE

MONDAY	TUESDAY

WEDNESDAY	THURSDAY

FRIDAY	SATURDAY	SUNDAY

GLOSSARY

Arbitration: An alternative dispute resolution (ADR) for divorcing couples who agree to have their case heard by a qualified arbitrator outside of court. This decision is typically binding, avoiding the need to enter the traditional court system.

Community Property State: Many know this as a "fifty-fifty" state, where assets are divided equally, and so are liabilities. As of 2025, these states include Arizona, California, Idaho, Louisiana, Nevada, New Mexico, Texas, Washington, and Wisconsin.

Collaborative Divorce: A team of professionals helps a divorcing couple settle without court proceedings. These professionals may include collaborative attorneys, financial specialists, CDFAs, divorce coaches, psychologists, realtors, etc. The goal is to have a legally binding final agreement reviewed by a judge.

Discovery: The process of gathering and sharing information between parties. In a divorce proceeding, this can include physical documents like titles, statements, as well as taking part in depositions and requests for information.

Depositions: Testimony, sworn and given out of court, to help gather information for a legal proceeding, or preparation for a trial.

Equitable Distribution State: During a divorce in this state, assets and liabilities are reviewed and split by the court in a way considered fair, but not always equitable. Often considered the opposite of a community property state.

Financial Affidavit: A statement listing an individual's financial situation, including flows of income, expenses, assets, and liabilities. This information is often used for determining the property settlement in a divorce, as well as alimony and expenses for children.

Legal Separation: A formal agreement when a couple lives and maintains their life separately instead of filing for and completing a divorce. They remain legally married. This type of separation is not always formally recognized in every state. As of 2025, Delaware, Florida, Georgia, Mississippi, Pennsylvania, and Texas do not have a formal system to recognize the same.

Litigation: The use of the public court system to hear complaints and review evidence, which might lead to a trial, so that unresolved disputes can be resolved.

Mediation: An alternative dispute resolution (ADR) method where a neutral mediator works as a facilitator to help a divorcing couple come to a resolution in their divorce settlement. The mediator does not make a binding decision.

No-Fault (Divorce): A divorce when there is no need to identify why the marriage was no longer viable, or which spouse had a responsibility for the breakdown of the marriage (i.e., adultery, abuse, etc.). Many times, mutual consent or a period of separation is needed. Consult your state's restrictions.

Petition for Divorce: This is usually the first step in formally applying for dissolution of the marriage. This is filed with the court and served to notify the opposing spouse formally.

Property Settlement Note: Written, agreed-upon details, when there may not be enough liquid assets to satisfy the settlement of a divorce.

Qualified Domestic Relations Order (QDRO): An order that instructs a retirement plan to pay funds to an identified party (i.e., child support, marital property to a former spouse, etc.).

Rehabilitative Maintenance: Financial support arranged to help support a spouse taking some time for education or to reestablish their earning capabilities.

Residency (Requirements for Divorce): Rules on how long a spouse/party must reside in a state before they can file for divorce according to the state's rules.

Temporary Orders: Court orders issued temporarily in a divorce while final settlement or judgment is agreed upon.

Uncontested (Default) Divorce: A divorce when all parties agree on all terms of the separation, including property division, child custody, and support.

Waiting Periods (for Divorce): A period, usually between the petition for divorce and finalization, that couples must wait before filing for divorce.

ABOUT THE AUTHOR

Donna Jean Kendrick's life transformed when she blended her family with Jim's, creating a bustling household of six children. As the founder of Sephton Financial, she already specialized in supporting families through significant transitions such as widowhood and divorce. However, her own experience of re-marriage and blending families deeply enriched her understanding and fueled her passion for helping others navigate similar challenges.

After the sudden death of her first husband, Greg, when she was just forty years old, Donna faced the daunting task of securing her family's financial future while managing her grief and supporting her three young children. This profound personal challenge revealed her calling: to assist families in transition to ensure they feel financially secure and supported.

With Jim, Donna found love again and encountered the complex realities of merging two families with distinct needs and financial implications. This journey inspired her to write *A Guide for Blended Families*, where she leverages her professional expertise and personal insights to help others smoothly combine their lives and finances. In this book, Donna provides practical advice, empathetic stories, and actionable steps to empower families to thrive together in their new configurations. Learn more at www.donnajeankendrick.com.

in linkedin.com/in/donna-kendrick

f facebook.com/DonnaJeanKendrick

instagram.com/@DonnaJeanKendrick

tiktok.com/@DonnaJeanKendrick

ABOUT THE PUBLISHER

Founded in 2019, Highlander Press is a vibrant, mid-sized publishing house dedicated to transforming the world through the power of words. We are deeply committed to diversity and bringing big ideas to the forefront. At Highlander Press, we help authors navigate the journey from initial concept through writing, editing, and publishing, culminating in the release of a book that not only fulfills a lifelong dream but also solidifies their expertise and boosts their confidence.

Our unique approach centers on forging strong, collaborative relationships with women-owned businesses across the publishing spectrum, including graphic design, marketing, launching, copyright management, and publicity. We believe in the power of community and operate by the mantra, "a rising tide lifts all boats." This philosophy not only enhances our business model but also ensures that our authors receive unparalleled support and opportunities to succeed.

Join us in making a mark in the literary world, where your voice is heard, and your message has the power to change lives.

in linkedin.com/company/highlander-press

f www.facebook.com/highlander press

◎ www.instagram.com/highlanderpress

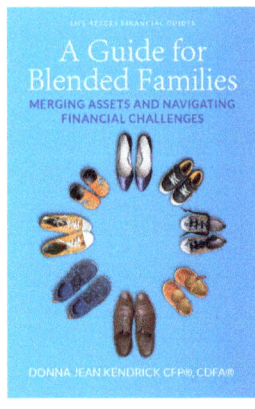